Alan Wong's New Wave Luau

Alan Wong's
NEW WAVE LUAU

Recipes from Honolulu's Award-Winning Chef

with John Harrisson

Photography by Danna Martel

TEN SPEED PRESS
Berkeley, California

Food photography copyright © 1999 by Danna Martel. Black-and-white photography on pages i and x–xxii by Danna Martel, Camera Hawaii.

Historical photographs on pages ii–iii, iv–v, xxiv–1, 2, 13, 22–23, 24–25, 40, 46–47, 48–49, 54, 55, 66–67, 68–69, 72–73, 82–83, 84–85, 97, 100, 101, 104–105, 106, 110, 124–125, 126, 140–141, 142, 162–163, 164, 170–171, 172–173, 174, 186, and 197 appear courtesy of the Bishop Museum, Honolulu, Hawaii.

Artifact photography on pages 26, 52, 59, 117, 132, 138, 168, and 179 by Jonathan Chester, Extreme Images, Berkeley. These artifacts include koa wood bowls, Hawaiian antiquities, and gourds that have been lovingly selected by JoAnn Deck, Narsai David, and Veni David. Endpapers: Hawaiian koa wood demi-lune tables from the royalty period. Koa wood and artifacts pictured here are the Property of an East Bay Gentleman.

TEN SPEED PRESS
P.O. Box 7123
Berkeley, California 94707
www.tenspeed.com

Distributed in Australia by Simon and Schuster, in Canada by Ten Speed Press Canada, in New Zealand by Southern Publishing Group, in South Africa by Real Books, in Southeast Asia by Berkeley Books, and in the United Kingdom and Europe by Airlift Books.

Jacket and book design by Nancy Austin
Petroglyph illustrations by Diana Reiss

Library of Congress Cataloging-in-Publication Data on file with publisher.

First printing, 1999
Printed in Singapore

1 2 3 4 5 6 7 8 9 10 — 03 02 01 00 99

This book is dedicated to my mom, born Tetsuko Anbo, now called Terry, and known affectionately in the restaurant as "Mom."

Her courage, love, and great cooking continue to inspire me.

CONTENTS

PREFACE

When I first met Alan Wong, I felt a little like Lois Lane meeting Clark Kent. It was 1989 and Alan was the chef for Mauna Lani Bay Hotel and Bungalows' new Canoe-House Restaurant on the Big Island of Hawaii.

I was the food writer planning the initial "Cuisines of the Sun" culinary celebration at the hotel. While I had handpicked the other participating chefs (Norman Van Aken, Bradley Ogden, and Robert Del Grande), I was "given" Alan, as he was selected by hotel management to represent the resort.

Ever the skeptical journalist, I had my qualms about Alan fitting into this high-profile mix. At that time, many hotel chefs were "meat-and-potato" cooks hired to please the masses rather than to create imaginative fare.

Alan came out of the kitchen to greet me. He was shy, soft-spoken… well, he reminded me of a culinary Clark Kent. I sighed and sat down to supper.

I still can recall every course of the elaborate dinner Alan prepared. Most of all, I remember my surprise. I couldn't believe that this mild-mannered person was the larger-than-life talent who drew such a bold signature on a plate. I don't know where the phone booth was, but Alan was no Clark Kent. Superman clearly ruled in the CanoeHouse kitchen, and now, of course, he thrives at Alan Wong's Restaurant.

Alan's cuisine defies an easy description. The flavors are astonishing, and like the crown to a king, they belong only to him. Like many chefs, Alan blends Asian and Western ingredients and culinary techniques, but he approaches food with a Hawaiian eye, soul, and palate.

In particular, Alan's cuisine celebrates the melting pot of cultures flourishing in the Aloha State. It trumpets homegrown ingredients, many from boutique purveyors few other chefs take the time or have the ingenuity to source. His food is complex yet seamless, rich but humble, whimsical and serious, at the same time.

Perhaps such finesse is achieved

because Alan himself is an amalgam, being of Japanese, Chinese, and Hawaiian ancestry. Maybe it's because of Alan's superior culinary training—an apprenticeship at Greenbrier, and a stint at Lutèce under the tutelage of legendary chef André Soltner.

My guess is that his star quality is a result of all of the above, and a little more. Underneath that modest demeanor is a man who demands perfection, yet only from himself. Not for the glory, or for the material rewards such precision can bring, but for the sake of the culinary art itself. And, he's determined to consistently delight his loyal clientele.

Over the past decade, I've savored many of Alan's creations. I've relished countless dishes at "Cuisines of the Sun," since Alan is the only chef to have participated in all nine years of the ongoing event. As the "Cuisines" coordinator, I consistently rely on Alan as a serious brainstorming partner. Quite frankly, I don't think I could do it without him.

Of course, he's perpetually late when it's time for the chefs to turn in menus for the event. I often threaten, tongue in cheek, that I will no longer include him in the many articles I write about Hawaii if he keeps missing my deadlines. But I know that's impossible. Alan's inclusion is a given. Not because he is my friend, but because his talent deserves recognition.

When creating "Cuisines of the Sun" 1993—"Hot Islands: Flavors from Four Worlds"—I envisioned a traditional luau with a contemporary spin. I knew only Alan could execute it. I tossed him the "new wave luau" idea and he flew with it.

July 17, 1993, was an electric night at Mauna Lani Bay. Under the hotel's famed milo tree, Alan and a legion of cooks crafted oyster shooters with wasabi "pearls" and tomato water infusion, spooned seaweed-crusted ahi poke over crostini, and built "nachos" of seared salmon and wasabi smashed potatoes.

The evening air was perfumed with ginger and coconut and mango. The food was wild and wonderful. Everyone loved it. The luau as we once knew it had been turned upside down and inside out, and, when spoken in the same breath as the name Alan Wong, would never possess the same meaning again.

Of course, I didn't know that this "Cuisines" extravaganza would spark the title of Alan's first cookbook. Now, with *New Wave Luau*, a bigger audience will discover the talent that many of us have admired so long. In the aloha spirit, I urge you to not only enjoy your copy of this cookbook, but to give one to a friend. For each recipe is in itself a present, an exquisite gift delivering boundless culinary joy.

—*Janice Wald Henderson*

ACKNOWLEDGMENTS

There are so many people I would like to thank. Some have made major contributions to this book; others have helped me in my career and made Alan Wong's the restaurant it is today. Better get started!

For making this book possible, I would like to thank Phil Wood, Jo Ann Deck, Mariah Bear, Nancy Austin, and the entire team at Ten Speed Press for making a dream turn into reality.

John Harrisson not only put the recipes and my vision into words but

Back row: *John Harrisson, Mark Okumura, Danna Martel, and Adam Jung.* **Front row:** *Sean Nakamura, Steven Ariel, Alan Wong, Lance Kosaka, and Barbara Stange.*

also captured the spirit and essence of the restaurant. We certainly shared many episodes during the course of putting this book together! I also feel like I have made a friend for life. We finally got it done, John!

Danna Martel brought her impres-

sive talent as a photographer to the project. I thank her for her special touch, tireless enthusiasm, and for giving it her all. Special thanks to Errol DeSilva and the staff of Camera Hawaii, including assistant Adam Jung.

I am grateful to Francis Higa for having enough confidence in my abilities to open Alan Wong's, and to Dan Nakasone and Kit Warrington for introducing me to Francis.

Thanks also to my board of directors at Alan Wong's—Craig Kobayashi, Lynn Nakamura, and Conrad Nonaka—for all their guidance and support.

I had a lot of help opening Alan Wong's, and today its success is still due to the strength of our team members. Charly Yoshida, the general manager, who came with me from the Big Island, oversees the service staff and takes care of our wine program. Mona Taga, our office manager, takes care of the administrative things, organizes my schedule, and makes my life a lot easier. My team of sous chefs—Steven Ariel, Barbara Stange, Karen Altherr, and Lance Kosaka—are each special in his or her own way. They're truly the next generation. Mark Okumura, our pastry chef, contributed greatly to this book with his dessert recipes, and he possesses an ideal palate for the tastes of our local clientele. Sean Nakamura, our beverage manager, also contributed to this book with his creative drink recipes. This bunch represents our management team, and I am so proud of them and thankful for all their loyalty, dedication, and hard work.

Next, I'd like to thank the rest of the kitchen: Marlowe Arcelona, Brian Doi, Abigail Langlass, Jon Matsubara, Gary Matsumoto, Jeffery Nakasone, Mark Silva, Nathan Tasato, Wade Ueoka, Brett Villarmia, and "Mom." These people are the backbone of the restaurant, unselfishly working long hours and always going the extra distance.

Likewise, the service staff: restaurant manager Mark Shishido, Les Arakaki, Jan Ashlock, Daniel Daly, Julie Enomoto, Asa Hartney, Glenn Horio, Brendan Jackson, Theresa Kondo, Monica Kong, Brian Kurata, Jeff Larsen, Eric Leung, Krissi Miller, Athena Mishima, Loren Nakaoka, Gayne Nitta, Robin Okawa, Eugene

The restaurant staff at their luau retreat.

Shimamura, Ryan Shindo, Larry Shomida, Kathleen Tagawa, Kan Wat, Beverly Wong, Jacky Wu, and Scot Yamamoto. Service is the vital key to the success of any restaurant and often makes or breaks the dining experience. These individuals are the first and last impression of our restaurant, and I must say that they do a great job.

In the office: Sui Lan Wong and Joan Kawamoto. Although behind the scenes, they provide us with tremendous support. They are also the friendly voices you hear when calling the restaurant.

On the farm: Kurt and Pam Hirabara, not only for their passion for growing beautiful produce, but also for being true friends and part of our family.

Without this great staff and cast of characters, I would not have my restaurant or this book, which is a product of their efforts and energies. I thank everyone associated with the restaurant for providing the setting in which we cook, create, taste, and come up with these innovative recipes.

INTRODUCTION

I am often asked how I got to cook in the style that I do—a style that has been variously described as Hawaii Regional Cuisine, East-West, Pacific Rim Fusion, and Euro-Asian. To start with, my ancestry is a mixture of Japanese, Chinese, and Hawaiian; I was born in Tokyo and grew up in Hawaii from the age of five. My culinary training in the mainland United

Helping mom in the kitchen, age four.

States was a mixture of American and European cuisine, heavily reliant on European techniques, and the years I spent in the kitchen at Lutèce in New York City were a great French experience. Combining this kind of professional background with the wonderful Hawaiian ingredients and cooking traditions that I returned to when I came back to the islands in 1986, it seemed a natural progression to cook in a cross-cultural style.

My mom wanted me to be a doctor, but what I really wanted to be was a professional baseball player. I grew up playing in the streets, and looking back, I feel very fortunate that organized sports kept me on the right side of the street, kept me out of trouble, and gave me my first true passion. I continued to play organized baseball until I was 25 years old, and I always wanted to coach a baseball team. The restaurant business doesn't allow that because you are always cooking dinner, but I got a taste of coaching during a year of teaching at culinary school, and today I am both coach and trainer in the restaurant kitchen. I make reference to those days I spent playing ball because many of the lessons I learned then serve me well today: the benefits of hard work, practice, commitment, discipline, and, when necessary, self-sacrifice. Sports taught me how to balance work with play, how to win and lose gracefully, and how to never give up. Perhaps most important of all, team sports made me understand that the team is more important than the individual. These lessons are the foundation of my style of coaching in the kitchen.

I inherited a love of food and an appreciation of flavorful, good-tasting home cooking from my family. My Chinese paternal grandfather always cooked for the family, and he was an excellent cook. My Japanese mother raised me on wonderful Japanese cooking. It was interesting to see my mom's style of cooking evolve as she learned about Western cooking after we moved to Hawaii. Being raised in the cultural melting pot of Hawaii, you get exposed to a wide range of ethnic foods. My warmest memories of growing up, besides home cooking, were the picnics at the beach, the backyard hibachi barbecues, and the potlucks where all the uncles and aunties tried to outdo each other. At the dinner table, whether it was my grandfather's house or at home with Mom, the food was never extravagant, but it always tasted good. I may not have realized it then, but today I know that I appreciate good food and flavors because of these early experi-

I am fortunate to have known Alan Wong since he was a young chef. My first impression was how naturally talented he was. From the very first, he was eager to learn the basics of classical cuisine, and he thoroughly mastered the techniques and lessons that came his way in the kitchen at Lutèce.

I think that what has impressed me the most about Alan over the years is his ability to adapt these fundamentals and his innate sense of flavor to the unique foods of Hawaii in dazzling style. Alan clearly revels in his own environment and culture; he is a tireless and remarkable culinary ambassador of his home state.

I enjoy dining at Alan Wong's restaurant in Honolulu not only because his cooking reflects the kind of man he is—lovely, serious, yet with a lighter side—but also because he has stuck to the basics he knows so well, and I admire that. Alan has never lost sight of the fundamental things that are all-important.

—Chef André Soltner, formerly of Lutèce in New York

ences. Mom comes to cook at my restaurant kitchen on weekends. She keeps the young ones in line, teaching them to utilize everything; being from the old school, she never wastes any food. Most importantly, she cooks the staff meal once in a while. When she cooks Japanese food, it both comforts me and gives the cooks a better understanding of my early inspirations.

My mom still can't believe that cooking is my profession because I was such a picky eater as a child. When I was in the fourth grade, our teacher made us eat all our vegetables for lunch, but the only ones I liked were corn, peas, and tomatoes. Anything else would almost make me gag, I hated them so much. I tried to

convince the teacher I was allergic, but of course that didn't work. Next, I figured I would hide the vegetables I didn't like in my empty milk carton. That worked for a few days. After that, I was reduced to stuffing the vegetables into my pants pockets, which worked fine for carrots and celery sticks but was less effective for creamed spinach, watery coleslaw, and clothes-staining pickled beets. Looking back, it was quite hilarious: I would come home from school, change into my baseball uniform, then hear Mom screaming at me because she would be washing my pants and pulling out all those vegetables! It was only after I left high school that I chose to expand my food horizons and gave vegetables a chance. As for cooking, my first serious attempt involved instant saimin noodles at age 13. My next venture was boiling

myself a hot dog, which ended with an explosion and one ugly ball of meat. Not a promising start, all in all.

Most summers I worked in the pineapple fields around my home town, Wahiawa. I got my first taste of the restaurant business one year when I worked as a dishwasher at Don the Beachcomber restaurant at the Waikiki Beachcomber Hotel. After graduating from high school, I returned to the Beachcomber Hotel as a dishwasher to earn my way through the University of Hawaii. At this point in my life, I developed the passion for curiosity and learning. This newfound passion got me promoted to busboy,

then to waiter, host, and restaurant cashier. Curious about hotel operations, I decided to leave food and beverage and became a front desk clerk and cashier. After a year, I returned to the restaurant as an assistant manager. After doing this for a year, my passion for learning told me that I needed to go to culinary school.

I got interested in cooking professionally in an unusual way. My fishing buddy, Wally Nishimura, a sous chef at The Beachcomber Hotel, got me inspired about cooking through carving ice. I started out by watching him work while I swept the fallen ice from his feet. One day he let me try. The turn-on for me was that I finally found something I could do with my hands other than playing baseball. Next, Wally showed me how to carve

vegetables and sculpt tallow. After work, while fishing or diving on the North Shore, we would discuss cooking, fishing, and culinary school. I was lucky to have a friend like Wally who was willing to be a mentor for an inquisitive country boy like me.

My first class in culinary school at Kapiolani Community College (KCC) in Honolulu was baking and cold food pantry. I can still vividly remember baking my first bread, my first pie, and making my first salad dressing. I felt as though a whole new world had opened up to me. I realized there was an ocean of knowledge I had to absorb and learn.

I remember my first job as a cook in a coffee shop called The Veranda at the Waikiki Beachcomber Hotel. This was an important first step because in order to keep up with the high volume I had to be organized, efficient, fast, and clean. I moved on to the Waialae Country Club, and meanwhile graduated from KCC. After working for a couple of years, I became restless. It was the same passion for curiosity and learning that I felt when I was a dish-

washer, only this time it was all about my culinary world. I knew I needed to learn more and that I needed to do it away from Hawaii.

I got accepted as an apprentice at The Greenbrier Hotel in White Sulphur Springs, West Virginia; it was as though I was in a different world. The food products were different, the menu terminology was new to me, all of a sudden I was a minority, and initially, I was lost. Luckily, I met Rod Stoner, the Greenbrier director of food and beverage. Mr. Stoner later helped me take my next step working in New York City, and he has always been an influential individual for me, and one to whom I still look for advice. I also met Mark Erickson, who was in charge of the apprenticeship program. Mark helped me to develop an eye for things. At that time, he was striving to win a place on the U.S. Culinary Olympic team. His experience on that team showed me a great deal about the culinary arts, presentation, and technique. The Greenbrier years were eye-opening in the culinary sense and also taught me valuable life lessons. Greenbrier taught me to cope, to adjust, and to persevere. It was my first taste of what it was like to live and breathe food.

Before graduating from the apprenticeship program, I flew up to New York City and met Rod Stoner's friend, Mark Sarrazin, who took me on a tour of Manhattan's better hotels and restaurants. By then, my dream was to work for André Soltner at Lutèce. Lutèce was the last stop on Mark's tour, and I finally met Chef Soltner. He told me, "I will hire you, but I don't have an opening right now." He told me that if I wanted to wait for an opening, I would have to move to New York first. That was enough for me, and so I made the jump, taking a job at the Ritz Carlton on Central Park South. Looking back,

I realize how gullible I was, thinking it would be easy to find a place to live in the city and not realizing how expensive or how big it really is. I didn't have a clue about how to get around. It was pure luck that I survived, and after living there for three months, Chef Soltner took me on. My dream had finally come true. Beginning in 1983, at age 26, I worked a formative three years at Lutèce.

It was at Lutèce that I learned the most about quality ingredients and a respect for food. I saw passion, and as a result, my passion for cooking grew even stronger. At Lutèce, I gained a better understanding for the basics, the foundation of cooking. An important lesson Chef Soltner taught me was to always remember the fundamentals of cooking and never to get

carried away. He put it this way: Cook with both feet on the ground; it just is not possible to cook with one foot in the air. Cooking on one foot is how he viewed some of the more outlandish cooking styles and "fusion" (confusion?) cuisines that were in vogue at the time. It's the same lesson as the biblical parable about building a house safely on rock rather than building rashly on sand.

Something that always particularly impressed me about Chef Soltner was his genuine humility and modesty. Although he was at the peak of his profession, and his restaurant was so highly rated, he still liked to describe himself as a "humble soup merchant" or no more than a skilled craftsman. He was a real "working boss," and during the hours the restaurant was open, I never saw him leave the kitchen. To this day, the Lutèce experience has influenced me the most in cooking philosophy and in my understanding of food. The chef de cuisine at Lutèce was Christian Bertrand, who also taught me a lot about cooking and for whom I have the utmost respect.

Despite having my dream job in New York City, deep down inside, I knew Hawaii was my home. I longed for the people, the food, my family, and my friends, and so I made the decision to return. Coming back to Hawaii was a big adjustment for me. I found myself working in hotels and also in hotel management, and I realized that the missing ingredient that the cooks were consistently hungry for was training. I found myself really enjoying teaching and training. One day I was contacted by my alma mater, Kapiolani Community College, to work as an instructor for their food service program. I had always appreciated the power of good teaching (and good coaching in sports), and I had always envisioned teaching one day. Now, I had the opportunity, so I accepted the offer. I learned a lot during my year teaching at KCC—about patience, the importance of good communication, and the power of good attitude, which in the professional kitchen can be more valuable than knowledge or skill. I also came to appreciate that making mistakes are an essential part of students' learning process and that we all learn at different rates and in different ways. Most of all, I realized that if a student does poorly, maybe he didn't fail; maybe the instructor failed as a teacher and communicator.

I knew that if I stayed in teaching any longer, it would be very hard to

THE RESTAURANT AS FAMILY: SOME PERSONAL OBSERVATIONS

In working with Alan to compile his unique collection of recipes and insights into the foods of Hawaii, I have been enormously impressed by the validity of Alan's philosophy that teamwork and family spirit—captured in the Hawaiian word *ohana*—make all the difference. The ambiance at Alan Wong's stems, in my opinion, from Alan's belief that a positive, committed attitude and a passion for excellence is even more important than knowledge or experience. This is something he learned from André Soltner when he worked at Lutèce. Alan encourages an open environment where learning and education is provided with the purpose of allowing individuals to further their personal development and careers. In return, he expects commitment, a positive attitude, and an openness to learning new things. When I asked Alan about the family atmosphere and the working dynamic at this restaurant that is unlike any I have encountered, Alan encouraged me to discuss it with his staff.

"Alan has a reputation for being a perfectionist and pretty intense," observes sous chef Barbara Stange. "In fact, his nickname is 'Mr. I'—'I' for intense—but really it's more his passion showing through. His reputation can be a bit intimidating for newcomers, but he really opens up when you get to know him. He is very caring and understanding, a great teacher, and I think of him almost like a brother. Alan likes to challenge his staff; he pushes our creativity and tries to make routine jobs interesting. We have fun here—we wouldn't put in the long hours we do if that wasn't true, and if we weren't proud of our results."

In the words of Charly Yoshida, general manager at Alan Wong's, "Alan views the restaurant staff as his family. As with any family, the relationship is a two-way commitment. You give Alan 100 percent, and he will show his gratitude and he will look out for you. He's always there if you need him. Alan is the best teacher and motivator I've ever known, and he derives a lot of satisfaction from seeing people learning and 'getting' it. He motivates by example, and he constantly takes time to attend to details."

Mark Okumura, pastry chef, credits Alan for helping him move forward in his career. "Alan made me focus on my goals and then encouraged me to set them higher and higher. That's how we got our retail chocolate business off the ground."

Lance Kosaka is a sous chef who began his career at Alan Wong's as a dishwasher. "I think of Alan more as a father or mentor than a boss, and Charly is like an uncle to us," he says. "Alan has let Barbara, Steven, and I develop the 'Next Generation Dinners,' where once a week or so, one of us cooks a menu of our choosing composed of dishes that we create. Guests can order our dinner, or order from the regular menu. It's a big confidence boost and a sign of trust in us. At the same time, Alan makes it clear that we have to earn that trust and keep working hard. In that sense he's more like a coach. I used to make more money when I was working in the construction business, but no amount of money can buy the feeling I have here. Sure, sometimes we have our differences in the kitchen, like any close-knit family, but Alan always helps us resolve them. He tells us, 'If there's never conflict, then no one cares.' We do care—I think we all share Alan's passion."

Sous chef Steven Ariel began working with Alan because he was impressed with his culinary style. Then, the more he got to know Alan, the more he appreciated that the learning process Alan initiated was not limited to the kitchen. "The more I put in, I realized the more I got out," says Steven. "The emphasis is on the team, both in the kitchen and in the restaurant as a whole. Alan includes us in certain decisions, such as scheduling and menu changes, and it's a democratic process, although ultimately, we know who's the boss. It's like nothing I've experienced before, and the mutually supportive atmosphere here is very rewarding. It makes me want to do for young chefs in the future what Alan has done for me and for all of us here at the restaurant."

—*John Harrisson*

return to cooking professionally, which was my real passion. So when I was approached by the Mauna Lani Bay Hotel and Bungalows on the Kohala Coast of the Big Island to be the opening chef for a new Pacific Rim–style restaurant called The CanoeHouse, I said yes. Hawaii Regional Cuisine was about to become a recognized culinary force in the state and beyond, and the time was just right for The CanoeHouse to play a role in establishing and advancing this exciting trend. I opened the ocean-front restaurant in June 1989, and the next few years I spent there were, without doubt, my most creative and rewarding experience up until that point. I realized that all the education and training I had gone through were designed for this specific opportunity. Now I finally had the chance to develop my own style of cooking.

After a few years at the CanoeHouse, I also took on Le Soleil, formerly the hotel's French restaurant. I was asked to create East-West food or Hawaii Regional Cuisine with a Mediterranean and French twist. Working at both The CanoeHouse and Le Soleil helped me define and refine my cooking style. Of course, the menus shared some similarities, but I also used distinctly different ingredients and techniques in each. I like to think of my cooking style at The CanoeHouse as based on the multi-ethnic food I was raised on, using Asian noodles, rice, peanut oil, rice wine vinegar, ginger, chiles, soy sauce, lemongrass, kaffir lime leaves, and other Asian products. At Le Soleil, it was based on the Western-oriented foods I was professionally trained to cook, using, by comparison, Italian noodles, potatoes, olive oil, balsamic vinegar, sundried tomatoes, basil, and oregano, although I was always seeking to give dishes an Asian twist. As time went by, I gained a greater sense of balance and a clearer focus, and I relished the creative process. Dishes not only had to taste good, but all the ingredients had to marry well, ideally with contrasts of flavor, texture, temperature, and sweetness and acidity. While trying new combinations, I had to be sure to cook with both feet on the ground, as Chef Soltner would say.

At the Mauna Lani Bay Hotel I was also given the unique opportunity of participating in the "Cuisines of the Sun" event, held every July. This celebration of food and wine from sunny climates brought many well-known chefs as well as a large and savvy audience to the Big Island. Themes of the event ranged from the cuisines of Florida and California,

Southeast Asia, the south of France, the Mediterranean, the Caribbean, India, Mexico, and Malaysia. "Cuisines of the Sun" is organized by Janice Wald Henderson, who asked me each year to be the "chameleon." My job was to be flexible and to cook according to that year's particular theme, but always in an East-meets-West context. This meant that I was cooking with ingredients and in a style I wouldn't normally think of or choose. The creative process this demanded resulted in some dishes that I am very proud of. One year, I prepared a meal for all the event participants that was called "The New Wave Luau"—traditional Hawaiian dishes transformed into a contemporary style—and that idea formed the basis for this cookbook.

Another milestone for me at the Mauna Lani Bay Hotel was being involved in the official formation of the group of energetic, exciting young chefs that came together to promote Hawaii Regional Cuisine. There are two primary objectives of the group: to promote Hawaii and the contemporary style of cooking found here today, and to help develop an agricultural network within the state by encouraging and supporting local

Among the awards we have received at Alan Wong's of which I am most proud are those given by *Honolulu* magazine. These coveted Hale'Aina awards are voted by the magazine's readers. When we won for Best New Restaurant in 1995 as well as Restaurant of the Year, I could hardly have been more thrilled. We were happy to have survived our first year and to be making progress, but to have won such recognition in doing so was almost unbelievable. Winning the Restaurant of the Year award again in 1996 also made me very proud because it meant that we had maintained our standards and kept our food and service at a consistently elevated level, which is a major challenge in the restaurant business. Likewise, when Alan Wong's

was nominated as Best New Restaurant in the country by the James Beard Foundation in 1996, the same year that the Foundation voted me as Chef of the Year in the Pacific and Northwest region, I was excited and honored. These awards are a tribute to the whole kitchen and to the entire dining-room and administrative staff, without whom our success would have been impossible. The 1997 Ilima Award given by the *Honolulu Advertiser* daily newspaper for Best Service was further vindication of our team effort and the leadership of our general manager, Charly Yoshida. We won the Hale'Aina award for Restaurant of the Year in 1998 and again in 1999, as well as the 1998 Ilima award for Favorite Hawaiian Restaurant.

Alan with Kurt and Pam Hirabara during the blessing of the land for their new farm in Waimea on the Big Island. The Hirabaras are part of the Alan Wong ohana *(family), and are among the many local growers the restaurant helps support.*

growers and farmers. These objectives have been successfully realized, and Hawaii is now internationally recognized as a culinary destination.

My time at the Mauna Lani Bay eventually led me to realize that I was ready to open my own restaurant. When the opportunity arose in Honolulu, I made the decision to take the next giant step. The seed was planted while working at Lutèce, and now my next dream was about to flower. After leaving the Big Island for Honolulu and many months of preparation and planning, I opened Alan Wong's in April 1995. We were fortunate to open to very positive reviews and have been blessed with a highly receptive and supportive audience. I think part of the reason for this success is that my food embraces so many of the different ethnic cooking traditions of Hawaii. My recipes feature the flavors that I grew up eating and the food that I love the best. Like me, Hawaii is truly a melting pot, and my goal for our guests is to give them a true slice of Hawaii.

What gives me even more satisfaction than such recognition and appreciation by the dining public is our success at the restaurant as a team. Our staff truly is the best I could ask for. They are hardworking, conscientious, loyal, and they give their all. Opening my own restaurant, I aimed to surround myself with talented, upbeat people, and I have been lucky in fulfilling that goal. I enjoy taking a nurturing role, bringing the staff along and building up their skills, creativity, and confidence. My philosophy has always been that it's the staff of any restaurant—both in the kitchen and front-of-house—that makes the difference. As I did on baseball fields growing up, we spend a lot of time team building and encouraging each staff member to achieve his or her goals.

Our focus is directed at the people who matter the most in this business, the guests who walk in our front door. The cornerstones of the restaurant are teamwork, quality, service, and hospitality. We even have a "professional trainer," Loren Lasher, who helps us develop skills in team building and employee education in all areas relating to guest satisfaction. Loren emphasizes problem solving, effective communication, character building,

self-esteem, and cooperation, enhancing all aspects of professional and personal development. I think this effort translates to a better dining experience, which ultimately is the philosophy of the restaurant.

The recipes in this book embody the spirit of the restaurant and the style in which I have been cooking ever since the CanoeHouse restaurant in the late 1980s. I like to think of this style as creative and fun, and I encourage you to be equally creative by experimenting with the recipes and substituting ingredients, whether out of choice or necessity. Play with the flavors in your own kitchen to suit your palate. Even though many of the recipes have multiple components, each of these elements also tastes great on its own, and you can use them in combinations of your choice. My definition of "cuisine" is when cooks begin to eat their own food. So keep tasting and retasting these recipes until the flavors work for you. I would like to think that these dishes will stretch your palate and exercise the senses.

"Talking story" with my friend Danny Akaka at the Eva Parker Woods Cottage at the Mauna Lani Bay Resort on the Big Island.

LOCAL FLAVOR

Above: *"Da girls"—Larissa, Ariana, Tiyana, and Kelsea—enjoying plate lunch in the back of my truck at the Rainbow Drive In, Honolulu.*

Left: *with my dad (right) and my good friend Conrad Nonaka (left), eating oxtail soup at the Kapiolani Bowling Alley.*

My nephews and niece, Justin (left), Keolani (center), and Christian (right), enjoying shave ice—a Hawaiian specialty—at the Matsumoto store in Haleiwa on Oahu's North Shore.

White rocks on a lava flow—a traditional way of sending messages.

Above: *Taking a breakfast break with the kitchen management team at Char Hung Sut, a local landmark in Honolulu's Chinatown.*

Left: *Taking a lunch break with the office management team at Ono Hawaiian Foods in Honolulu.*

Hawaii: The Culinary Melting Pot

Ever since Captain Cook's expedition of 1778, successive visitors and groups of immigrants have brought new ingredients, foods, and cooking styles to the islands. Each has contributed to the unique hybrid that is modern Hawaii Regional Cuisine—some more than others.

The first few decades following Cook's voyages brought major changes to the traditional Hawaiian diet. Livestock such as cattle and sheep were introduced, and all manner of new fruits and vegetables were brought by British and other European traders. In the early 1820s, American whalers and missionaries, mostly from New England, introduced their own style of cooking and ingredients such as beans, salted cod, and salmon. American businessmen and entrepreneurs followed in large numbers through the 1800s.

As the growing sugar industry required more plantation workers in the 1850s to replace the declining number of native Hawaiians, thousands of field laborers arrived from China, mostly from Canton and the south. In the late 1860s, there was a new wave of immigration, this time from Japan. In the late 1870s and early 1880s, large numbers of Portuguese laborers came to work in the pineapple fields, together with smaller groups of Germans and Norwegians. The continued demand from the sugar and pineapple industries during the first decade of the twentieth century saw significant waves of immigration from Korea and the Philippines, with smaller groups from Okinawa, Puerto Rico, Spain, Russia, and Samoa. Hawaii had become the crossroads of the Pacific and, in some senses, of the world. By the 1930s, Hawaiians of Japanese descent had become the largest single ethnic group, which remains the case today.

The effects of these new cultures on the cuisine of Hawaii was enormous. At first, the foods and cooking habits of each group remained localized. But over time, stores and restaurants offered a wider range of foods to an increasingly integrated population, and intermarriage between members of different ethnic groups meant that foods and cooking traditions became progressively mixed. In time, each new style became grafted onto the mainstream Hawaiian and *haole* (Caucasian) cooking. Asian ingredients, such as rice, noodles, soy sauce, miso, and various cabbages and greens, and new cooking styles, such as stir-frying and steaming, became an important part of the kitchens. The popularity of dim sum, wonton, sushi, and sashimi began to extend beyond traditional ethnic boundaries. Likewise, kim chee and Korean barbecue, Portuguese sweet bread, doughnuts, sausage, Filipino adobo dishes, and Samoan salt beef crossed culinary lines. Immigration in the 1960s and '70s from the Southeast Asian countries such as Vietnam and Thailand brought the flavors of those countries into the mainstream, too.

The result has been the development of "local food," a uniquely Hawaiian cuisine that represents a glorious and delicious mixture of many cultures. Aspects of this cuisine are detailed in the recipes that follow, many of which borrow and expand on these disparate foods, their long and eminent traditions, and their expressive flavors.

The New Wave Luau

The New Wave Luau

While most of the recipes in this book draw on native Hawaiian foods for everyday meals, this chapter focuses on the foods and traditions of the Hawaiian feast, the luau. The celebratory feast is as old as society in Polynesia, but you may be surprised that the term *luau* is a relatively recent invention, dating from the late 1820s, when European sailors and traders described the feasts they attended. No doubt the name arose because of the number of dishes featuring luau leaves, the young green taro tops that are always served at Hawaiian feasts. In the 1850s, a Honolulu newspaper, the *Pacific Commercial Advertiser*, began referring to "luaus," and the term became widely used and recognized.

Historically, what we call a *luau* was known as *aha'aina* (literally, meal gatherings); smaller parties were called *pa'ina*. *Aha'aina* were held for numerous reasons, just as luaus are today (see sidebar on page 13). Typical dishes would be kalua pig and mullet, to honor the god Lono; taro, which was believed to be Lono's plant form; shrimp; crab; and seaweed.

The first ruler who united all of the Hawaiian islands, King Kamehameha, who lived from 1758 to 1819, sometimes held celebrations that lasted for weeks. Later, King Kalakaua (1847–1891) often gave luaus at his royal palace in Honolulu for hundreds of people at a time, leading to his nickname of "the merry monarch." The luau was also the royal family's preferred method of displaying hospitality to visiting dignitaries. Local papers recorded a luau Kalakaua held in honor of the author Robert Louis Stevenson, who was visiting the islands. Princess (later Queen) Lili'uokalani hosted a luau in 1869 for the first visiting member of European royalty, Queen Victoria's son, Prince Alfred. The *Hawaiian Gazette* wrote that the luau was "the largest feast that has been spread for many years…every variety of Hawaiian food was offered, to the amusement of the distinguished guest." The Princess liked to hold luaus lasting from late morning until sunset. Typically, they featured entertainment consisting of ancient hulas and chants, and games that displayed Hawaiian athletic prowess. One report comments: "On these occasions people were served everything that can be roasted or fried almost until comatose, before being revived with ice cream." This last reference suggests that the luau had long been adapted to meet contemporary taste.

Descriptions of late-nineteenth century luaus mention flower leis given to welcome the guests and lacy maidenhair ferns strewn on the floor and tables stacked with pineapples, bananas, watermelons, mangoes, other fruits, and sugar cane. In front of each guest, a condiment dish contained ground kukui nut, red Hawaiian salt, chopped scallions, *limu* (seaweed), dried shrimp, and slices of dried fish. Coconut bowls placed around the table held lomi salmon, poi, fresh opihi, and squares of haupia in coconut cream. Large serving bowls held cooked sweet potatoes, taro leaves, and baked banana. The main luau dishes were served all at once: steaming hot kalua pig, poke, crabs, baby lobsters, fish baked in ti leaves, squid cooked in coconut milk, and cooked taro. Most of the food was eaten in a leisurely manner and with the hands. The highest compliment was "to suck one's fingers as audibly as possible," and to withdraw the fingers from the mouth with a satisfied smack in appreciation of the cuisine.

Today, the luau lives on, enjoyed by Hawaiians of all ethnic backgrounds. With the luau, we celebrate the spirit of *ohana* and family, and mark important passages and events in our lives. Alas, the luaus experienced by tourists are all too often pale imitations of the real thing. If you are fortunate enough to be invited to an authentic family luau, drop everything and go!

With the recipes in this chapter, I bring the traditional luau foods up to date and give them a new interpretation. If I were King of Hawaii for a day, I'd hold a luau just like they did in the last century. I'd invite my family and closest friends, and share these favorite dishes of mine, just as I hope you will share them with your guests. The main dishes and side dishes in this chapter can be mixed and matched in any combination. They can be prepared individually or as a large feast featuring many dishes. The recipes here serve four, but they can be doubled or tripled to fit the needs of your own luau.

Kalua Pig

Kalua Pig is perhaps the most traditional of all luau dishes. It is also invariably a key component of the Hawaiian Plate that you'll find at a local restaurant. It's interesting that similar barbecued pulled pork dishes are also traditional in countries with a Spanish or Portuguese heritage, such as Cuba, Mexico, and Brazil.

The traditional preparation of Kalua Pig involves a whole carcass, building an underground oven, and a 2-day timescale. The results are succulent and the elaborate process makes for a special occasion. Luckily, you can achieve acceptable results with the convenient method using a much smaller cut of pork, a regular oven, and about 2 hours. Both methods are provided here to let you make the call.

Traditional Method

Dig the imu, or underground oven, to a depth of 2 to 3 feet, and a little longer and wider than the pig to be roasted. Stack *kiawe* (mesquite) or guava kindling wood in the bottom of the *imu*, with larger firewood piled on top. Pile volcanic lava rocks on top of the wood; these are porous and the holes retain the heat, yet they will not crack when red hot. Light the wood and burn for 2 to 4 hours, or until the wood has burned and the rocks are red hot. Spread the coals evenly in the pit.

Meanwhile, thoroughly clean the pig. Its dressed weight will be about half of the "on the trotter" weight (average dressed weight usually ranges from 50 to 200 pounds). Shave or singe off the coarse hair. Hang and drain the carcass overnight. Salt the pig inside and out with Hawaiian rock salt. Stuff hot stones inside the stomach and foreleg cavities and tie the legs together.

Just before adding the pig to the *imu*, layer damp banana stumps and banana and ti leaves over the hot coals to create steam. Add the pig, belly up. Place additional damp banana and ti leaves over the pig, and then wet burlap bags to completely cover the pig, overlapping the edge of the *imu* (ancient Hawaiians used coconut cloth or matting). Add a layer of canvas to cover the burlap and to keep the steam inside. Cover the canvas with the dirt taken from the *imu* pit.

You can cook other foods with the pig, such as duck, chicken, turkey, fish, taro, breadfruit, and sweet potatoes. Cook a 50-pound pig for 2$\frac{1}{2}$ to 3 hours in the *imu*; a 200 pounder will take double that time. An important part of preparing the pig and waiting for it to cook—and sometimes the whole point of the exercise—is the shared family time, socializing, and partying that takes place while the pig cooks.

When the cooking time is up, carefully shovel the dirt from the canvas. Remove the layers of canvas, burlap, and leaves. Remove the stones from the pig's cavities. When cool enough, carve the pig and shred the meat.

Kalua is derived from the two Hawaiian words *ka* (the) and *lua* (hole), which refer to the *imu* or underground pit used for the oven. In ancient times, pig was often eaten as a ceremonial food, but it was *kapu*—forbidden—for women.

The Hawaiians were unique among Polynesian societies in deriving salt from seawater; it was used to cure meat and fish and as a seasoning. They made salt by using wide salt pans, *kaheka*, typically 6 feet in diameter and 6 inches deep, which were made of earth and lined with clay (sometimes natural rock basins were used). Seawater was poured in, using calabashes, or the salt pans were positioned at the high-tide mark. The water would be evaporated by the sun over a period of days, leaving salt. Traditionally, salt made on Kauai was mixed with red earth (containing iron), and this red salt is still served at luaus and celebrations. Hawaiian salt was traded extensively in the 19th century, in the days before refrigeration, and was a prized commodity.

Convenient Method

If you haven't the time or place for pit-steaming a whole pig, use this more convenient Kalua Pig recipe. For a further shortcut, substitute shredded smoked or roasted pork for the Kalua Pig in the recipes, but the flavors will be quite different. Be sure to use a brand of liquid smoke that contains no chemicals or preservatives, available at good natural foods grocery stores.

6 ti leaves, or 2 banana leaves
6 pounds pork butt, cut into 6 pieces about 2 inches thick
2 1/2 tablespoons Hawaiian or kosher salt
2 1/2 tablespoons all-natural liquid smoke flavoring

Preheat the oven to 500°.

Lay a piece of aluminum foil measuring 9 inches by 11 inches on a flat work surface. Place 3 ti leaves or 1 banana leaf on top of the foil, and the pork on top. Sprinkle with the salt and liquid smoke. Place the remaining 3 ti leaves or banana leaf on top of the pork. Cover with additional foil and seal tightly. Place the package in a large roasting pan, fill with 2 inches of water, and cover the pan with foil to seal in the steam.

Cook for 1 1/2 to 2 hours, or until tender. When cool, shred using 2 forks. Refrigerate for up to 5 days (or freeze) until needed.

YIELD: 8 CUPS

Ti leaves are long, narrow, dark green, smooth, and shiny. They were used by ancient Hawaiians to wrap, insulate, and flavor foods for cooking as well as for decorative purposes. The leaves were also important for clothing, roofing material, ritual ceremonies, and many other uses. Ti leaves are considered to bring good luck. Whenever I travel I put a ti leaf in each bag to make sure it gets there, and the method hasn't failed yet. You can also eat the root of the ti plant after it is steamed in the imu; natural sugars in the root make it taste very sweet. The plant, which was brought to Hawaii from Polynesia centuries ago, grows well in rich soil and plenty of moisture.

Kalua Pig Risotto with Two-Cabbage Slaw

Kalua Pig is well suited to a dish like risotto. In fact, it's difficult to go too far wrong using Kalua Pig anywhere you would use pork. The slaw makes a simple and attractive garnish for all kinds of dishes.

TWO-CABBAGE SLAW

^{1}/3 cup finely julienned carrots

^{1}/3 cup finely julienned red cabbage

^{1}/3 cup finely julienned green cabbage

1 tablespoon Slivered Scallions
   (page 175)

4^1/2 cups Chicken Stock (page 177)

1 tablespoon olive oil

^{1}/2 tablespoon minced garlic

^{1}/4 cup diced onion

1 (1-inch) piece ginger, smashed

1 cup Arborio rice

2 tablespoons white wine

Salt to taste

6 tablespoons fresh corn kernels

^{3}/4 cup Kalua Pig (page 4)

3 tablespoons quartered mixed
   mushrooms, such as shiitakes,
   oyster, and button

6 tablespoons finely diced fresh or
   canned water chestnuts

3 tablespoons butter

3 tablespoons truffle butter

6 tablespoons grated Parmesan cheese

^{1}/4 cup Lomi Tomato Relish
   (page 21)

In a bowl, combine the carrots, cabbages, and scallions. Refrigerate until needed.

In a saucepan, bring 2^1/2 cups of the stock to a boil. Meanwhile, in a sauté pan over medium-high heat, heat the olive oil. Sauté the garlic and onion for 2 minutes. Add the ginger and rice, stirring so the rice is coated evenly with the oil. Add the wine. Stirring constantly, add the hot stock to the rice, ^{1}/2 cup at a time, letting the rice absorb the liquid before adding more. Cook for 3 minutes after the last addition. Total cooking time from the first addition of the stock should be about 10 minutes. Season with salt.

In a large saucepan over medium-high heat, heat the remaining 2 cups of stock until just boiling. Add the corn and Kalua Pig and cook for 2 minutes. Add the mushrooms, water chestnuts, and cooked rice mixture. Cook for 3 minutes longer, or until the liquid is absorbed by the rice. Swirl in the butter, truffle butter, and cheese. Mix until the butter is melted and completely incorporated. Season with salt.

Divide among individual bowls. Garnish with the relish and slaw.

YIELD: 4 SERVINGS

"Surely, even before the arrival of the first Polynesian settlers all those centuries ago, there were some indigenous animals on the islands?" one of our restaurant guests asked recently. The answer is no. Even the wild boar that still roam the more inaccessible parts of the islands were introduced here by man. Hawaii has always been so isolated from other land masses that the only indigenous land mammals are bats. Given their small size and poor eyesight, it would be interesting to know how they got here!

Kalua Pig Kanaka Nachos

These nachos use local Hawaiian ingredients. The Lomi Tomato Relish, guacamole, and Refried Taro all make wonderful accompaniments to these nachos—especially together—but if pressed for time, you can prepare just one or two of the sides.

Vegetable oil for deep-frying

5 wonton wrappers, cut into quarters

20 deep-fried taro chips (page 44)

1 cup Kalua Pig (page 4)

1 cup shredded romaine lettuce

2 tablespoons shredded Monterey Jack cheese

^{1}/$_4$ cup mozzarella cheese

^{1}/$_4$ cup Refried Taro (page 21)

^{1}/$_4$ cup Lomi Tomato Relish (page 21)

^{1}/$_4$ cup Alan's Asian Guacamole (page 128)

4 teaspoons Hawaiian Chile Pepper Sour Cream (page 183), for garnish

^{1}/$_4$ cup cilantro sprigs, for garnish

Preheat the broiler.

In a deep fryer or large saucepan over high heat, heat about 3 inches of vegetable oil to 350°. Deep-fry the wonton wrappers for 2 to 2^1/$_2$ minutes, or until crisp and golden. Remove and drain on paper towels.

Arrange the taro and wonton chips on a heatproof platter. Top with the Kalua Pig, lettuce, and cheese. Place under the broiler until the cheese is melted. Accompany with the Refried Taro, Lomi Tomato Relish, and Alan's Asian Guacamole. Garnish with the sour cream and cilantro.

YIELD: 4 SERVINGS

Kanaka is a Hawaiian word dating from the nineteenth century meaning *local*, or native Hawaiian, and it was used to distinguish the indigenous population from the newcomers. In these more assimilated times, it's used much less.

One of the earliest written descriptions of a luau was contained in the journal of Richard Brinsley Hinds, published as *The Journey of the Voyage of the Sulphur*. In July 1837, Hinds was invited to a *louhow* in Manoa Valley (in what is now part of Honolulu). He records, not without some chauvinism, "It is said to be of native origin, and no doubt is, but has civilized customs grafted on it...I previously thought *louhow* meant baked dog but I think now that I was then in error. The essential part, and I believe the origin of the name, is the young leaves of the taro fixed in a particular manner, and which closely resembles spinach. A *louhow* must be cooked after the native fashion.... Visitors at a *louhow* must dispense with some of the luxuries of civilized society. The dinner is spread on a clean mat on the ground after the native fashion, and each person seating himself as he best can proceeds to work. In fact it is a Sandwich Island pic-nic."

Kalua Pig Caesar Salad in Crispy Cheese Baskets with Poi Vinaigrette and Anchovy Dressing

~~~~~~

In this recipe, the traditional Caesar salad meets the New Wave Luau. This dish is typical of how I create my recipes. I had tried several adaptations of the Caesar salad, but I was not completely satisfied with any of the results. Then one day, when I was hungry for a salad, I experimented with some of the sides and dressings already prepared for other dishes in the restaurant kitchen. First I added some Kalua Pig to the greens, then some of the Poi Vinaigrette that I use for the Kalua Duck (page 10). I sprinkled a little of the chile pepper vinaigrette and Caesar dressing over the salad, and presto: I had the salad of my dreams. (*Recipes containing uncooked eggs are not recommended for immuno-compromised individuals or small children.*)

ANCHOVY DRESSING

1 egg plus 1 yolk

5 anchovy fillets

1 teaspoon minced garlic

1 tablespoon red wine vinegar

1 teaspoon Worcestershire sauce

1 teaspoon Dijon mustard

1/2 tablespoon freshly squeezed lemon juice

1/2 cup water

1 cup olive oil

Salt to taste

POI VINAIGRETTE

1/4 cup poi

1/2 cup Infused Tomato Water (page 176)

1 tablespoon tarragon vinegar

2 tablespoons olive oil

1/2 teaspoon Chile Pepper Water (page 175)

CRISPY CHEESE BASKETS

4 cups grated Parmesan cheese

GARLIC CROUTONS

1 tablespoon butter

1 cup diced French bread

1/2 teaspoon minced garlic

Salt and pepper to taste

1/4 cup Tomato–Chile Pepper Vinaigrette (page 58)

24 baby romaine lettuce leaves

4 anchovy fillets

4 teaspoons finely grated Parmesan cheese

1 cup warm Kalua Pig (page 4)

To prepare the Anchovy Dressing, in a blender, combine the egg, yolk, anchovies, garlic, vinegar, Worcestershire sauce, mustard, lemon juice, and water. With the machine running, slowly add the oil until it is completely incorporated. Season with salt. Refrigerate until needed.

To prepare the Poi Vinaigrette, in a blender, combine the poi and tomato water and mix well. Add the vinegar and blend to incorporate. With the machine running, slowly add the olive oil until it is completely incorporated. Add the Chile Pepper Water and blend to incorporate. Refrigerate until needed.

To prepare the cheese baskets, sprinkle 1 cup of the cheese evenly in a 6-inch nonstick pan. Place over low heat for about 2 minutes, or until the cheese melts together into a sheet and begins to bubble. While still warm and pliable, drape over the end of an upturned tumbler or soda can. Mold the cheese so that it forms a basket; as it cools it will harden and keep its basket shape. Remove from the glass or can and invert. Repeat for the remaining 3 baskets.

To prepare the croutons, in a sauté pan over medium heat, melt the butter. Add the bread and sauté, tossing or stirring occasionally, for 3 to 4 minutes. Add the garlic and sauté for 1 minute longer. Season with salt and pepper.

To serve, drizzle 1 tablespoon each of the Anchovy Dressing, Poi Vinaigrette, and Tomato–Chile Pepper Vinaigrette around individual plates. Place a cheese basket in the middle of each plate and stand 6 lettuce leaves upright inside each basket. Drizzle 1 tablespoon of the Anchovy Dressing over the lettuce in each basket. Top with an anchovy fillet and 1 teaspoon of the grated cheese. Divide the Kalua Pig into mounds next to each basket. Garnish with the croutons scattered around. Accompany with the remaining Anchovy Dressing.

YIELD: 4 SERVINGS

Kalua Duck in Taro Pancakes with Poi Vinaigrette

Today, as in ancient times, duck, geese, and other fowl can be cooked in the *imu* together with, or instead of, pig or other meat. Because the traditional *imu* is somewhat time-consuming, I've designed a more convenient method. The duck retains all of its natural juiciness and develops a smoky flavor when cooked this way. You can substitute 1 pound of smoked duck meat, although the flavor will be different. The pancakes are a great way to enjoy taro. Store extra pancake batter in the refrigerator for up to 3 days, and use pancakes for other recipes or on their own.

6 ti leaves, or 2 banana leaves

1 (5- to 6-pound) duck

2¹/₂ tablespoons Hawaiian or kosher salt

2¹/₂ tablespoons all natural liquid smoke flavoring

TARO PANCAKES

8 ounces taro

2 cups milk

2 tablespoons cornstarch

2 eggs

1 cup flour

Salt and pepper to taste

4 teaspoons vegetable oil

¹/₂ cup Poi Vinaigrette (page 8)

2 tablespoons Tomato–Chile Pepper Vinaigrette (page 58)

¹/₄ cup Lomi Tomato Relish (page 21)

Pinch of black sesame seeds, for garnish

2 teaspoons Slivered Scallions (page 175), for garnish

Preheat the oven to 500°.

Lay a piece of aluminum foil measuring 9 inches by 11 inches on a flat work surface. Place 3 ti leaves or 1 banana leaf on top of the foil, and the duck on top of the leaf. Sprinkle with the salt and liquid smoke. Place the remaining 3 ti leaves or 1 banana leaf on top of the duck. Cover with additional foil and seal tightly. Place the package in a large roasting pan, fill with 2 inches of water, and cover the pan with foil to seal in the steam.

Cook for 1¹/₂ to 2 hours, or until fork tender. When cool, remove the duck meat and shred using 2 forks. Refrigerate for up to 4 days (or freeze) until needed.

To prepare the pancakes, place the taro in a steamer or vegetable basket set in a saucepan of lightly boiling water. Cover and steam for about 2 hours, or until completely tender.

In a blender, combine the steamed taro, milk, cornstarch, eggs, and flour and blend to form a batter. Season with salt and pepper. In a medium nonstick pan over medium-low heat, heat 1 teaspoon of the vegetable oil. Ladle in about 2 tablespoons of the batter and tilt the pan to spread it evenly. Cook the pancake until brown on each side. Keep warm while preparing the remaining 3 pancakes.

To serve, divide the pancakes among individual plates. Place the Kalua Duck in the middle of each pancake. Roll up the pancake. Drizzle both vinaigrettes around the plates. Top with the relish. Garnish with the sesame seeds and scallions.

YIELD: 4 SERVINGS

The most common type of taro grown in Hawaii is lehua taro, which is the best type for making poi; its pink flesh turns purple when cooked. Traditionally, poi (meaning "to pound") was made from steamed taro root by pounding with specially sculpted rocks on custom-made hardwood boards. Water was added to give the paste the desired consistency. Poi is associated with Hawaii rather than any other Pacific societies because the earliest settlers preferred to eat taro in this semiliquid form rather than as a steamed vegetable as served elsewhere. Other Polynesian societies also make poi with breadfruit and bananas. As far as I know, Alan Wong's is the only restaurant in the state that makes poi every night. For more on taro, see page 21.

Kalua Turkey Quesadillas with Minted Mango Relish and Hawaiian Chile Pepper Sour Cream

I enjoy Southwestern and Mexican cooking. This luau dish with a difference proves that these cuisines travel well. When I went to Santa Fe recently to participate in their annual Wine and Chile Fiesta, I discovered that merging cuisines works in any venue. Hawaii Regional Cuisine adapts very successfully to the styles of other regions, whether served in Honolulu, Santa Fe, or your home. Use Kalua Turkey left over from this recipe with Taro Pancakes (page 10) or to replace the meat in any of the Kalua recipes in this chapter. Alternatively, prepare using a 3-pound turkey breast instead of a whole turkey.

10 ti leaves, or 4 banana leaves

1 (6- to 8-pound) turkey

2 1/2 tablespoons Hawaiian or kosher salt

2 1/2 tablespoons all-natural liquid smoke flavoring

QUESADILLAS

2 tablespoons butter

1/2 cup quartered shiitake mushrooms

1/2 cup Boursin cheese

8 (6-inch) flour tortillas

1/4 cup Minted Mango Relish (page 133)

1/4 cup Hawaiian Chile Pepper Sour Cream (page 183)

12 sprigs cilantro, for garnish

Preheat the oven to 500°.

Lay a piece of aluminum foil measuring 9 inches by 11 inches on a flat work surface. Place half of the ti or banana leaves on top of the foil, and the turkey on top of the leaves. Sprinkle with the salt and liquid smoke. Place the remaining leaves on top of and around the turkey. Cover with additional foil and seal tightly. Place the package in a large roasting pan, fill with 2 inches of water, and cover the pan with foil to seal in the steam.

Cook for 1 1/2 to 2 hours, or until fork tender. When cool, remove the turkey meat and shred using 2 forks. Refrigerate for up to 5 days (or freeze) until needed.

To prepare the quesadillas, in a sauté pan or skillet over medium-high heat, melt the butter. Add the mushrooms and sauté for about 3 minutes, or until golden brown. Spread 1/2 tablespoon of the cheese on one side of each tortilla. Place about 1/4 cup of the turkey evenly over the cheese on 1 of the tortillas. Sprinkle 2 tablespoons of the cooked mushrooms over the turkey and top with another tortilla, cheese side down. Keep warm while preparing the remaining 3 quesadillas.

In a medium nonstick pan over medium heat, warm each quesadilla for 2 minutes on each side, or until the tortillas are slightly brown on the outside and hot inside. Cut into eighths.

To serve, divide the quesadilla pieces among individual plates. Top with the relish and sour cream. Garnish with the cilantro.

YIELD: 4 SERVINGS

Steamed Clams with Kalua Pig, Shiitake Mushrooms, and Spinach in "Da Bag"

Shortly before we opened Alan Wong's, I was visiting my mom and volunteered to help cook dinner. She asked me if I would steam some clams she had bought, and feeling creative, I decided to prepare them a little differently if I could. I looked around the refrigerator and pulled out some cooked Kalua Pig, spinach, and tomatoes. I added these to the clams and steamed everything together in a covered pan. The result was so successful, I decided to adapt it for the restaurant menu. Rather than cooking in a pan, I chose to cook the dish *en papillote*—the classic French method of baking food inside sealed parchment paper, which is how salmon was sometimes cooked at Lutèce. Instead of paper, I use foil bags. It's an impressive sight when this dish is carried to the table, with the puffed-up shiny envelope containing the sizzling ingredients. When the foil is pulled back and the steam and aroma escapes, everyone seems to want one!

1 tablespoon butter

2 teaspoons minced garlic

1/2 cup quartered shiitake mushrooms

2 cups firmly packed spinach

20 Manila clams, washed

2 cups Kalua Pig (page 4)

1/4 cup finely diced tomatoes

1 cup Chicken Stock (page 177)

Preheat the oven to 500°.

Cut 4 strips of 18-inch-wide heavy-duty gauge aluminum foil 40 inches long (or use 2 overlapping strips of 12-inch-wide foil). Form foil bags, with one end left open, by folding each strip of foil in half lengthwise and seal the sides by folding the edges over together 3 or 4 times.

In a sauté pan over medium-high heat, melt the butter. Add the garlic and sauté for 2 minutes, stirring occasionally. Add the mushrooms and sauté for 2 minutes longer.

In a saucepan of boiling salted water, blanch the spinach for 30 seconds. Transfer the spinach to an ice bath to cool. Drain and gently squeeze out any excess moisture.

Divide the clams, Kalua Pig, mushrooms, spinach, and tomatoes among 4 large ovenproof soup bowls (preferably 10 inches in diameter). Pour 1/4 cup of the stock into each bowl. Slide the bowls inside the foil bags. Pour 1 cup of warm water inside the bottom of each bag before sealing the open end. Carefully place the bags on a baking sheet. Bake for 15 minutes; steam created by the water inside the bag will puff up the foil and cook the ingredients inside. If possible, cook 2 bags at once and then repeat for the remaining 2 bags; reheat the bags cooked first just before serving. If the bags do not puff up, check for holes or leaks.

To serve, place the bags on individual plates. Cut open at the table. Be careful as hot steam will rise from the bag. Diners should discard clams that did not open during cooking.

YIELD: 4 SERVINGS

Another historic account of the luau was given by Captain F. W. Beechey, who visited Honolulu aboard H.M.S. *Blossom* in 1827. He wrote, "The King gave an entertainment, of which his guests were seated at a long table spread in the European style, and furnished with some very good wines. Among other good things we had Leuhow, a dish of such delicious quality that excursions are occasionally made to the plantations for the pleasure of dining upon it; and from this circumstance, a picnic and a Leuhow party have become nearly synonymous. The ingredients of this dish are the tops of the taro plant and mullet which have been fattened in the fishponds; these are wrapped in large leaves and baked in the ground, though sometimes fowls and pork are used."

THE TRADITIONAL HAWAIIAN FEASTS

Before the word *luau* was introduced in the nineteenth century, traditional feasts were known as *aha'aina*. Here are some examples of particular feasts:

aha'aina ainakomo: Initiation feast

aha'aina ho'okipa: Feast of hospitality; a spontaneous party organized to welcome returning relatives or long-absent friends. Failure to honor those returning could be considered an insult.

aha'aina ho'ola'a: Feast of dedication or consecration; for example, a house, canoe, church, or fishing net.

aha'aina laulima: Feast of countless hands, celebrated communal efforts such as clearing land, building fish ponds, preparing taro fields, or bringing in the taro harvest.

aha'aina makaluhi: Feast for tired persons, to honor those who helped prepare and serve the feast for others.

aha'aina make: Funeral feast, to comfort the mourners.

aha'aina male: Wedding feast or reception.

aha'aina mawaewae: Feast of the firstborn, celebrated within 24 hours of birth. A ritual held as a blessing for the child and as a "path clearing" for future siblings.

aha'aina palala: Informal feast, for friends and relatives of a firstborn bearing gifts for the newborn. Today's baby luaus continue this tradition.

aha'aina piha makahiki: Feast of the fullness of the year, held for anniversaries, especially for a firstborn's first birthday.

aha'aina piwai: Feast held to break the monotony of rural life.

aha'aina puka: Graduation feast.

By now you must realize that luaus are organized at the slightest provocation—and with good food and a good time guaranteed, why not?

Chicken "Hawaiian Plate" with Pipikaula and Lomi Salmon on Taro Leaf Sauce with Luau Lumpia

Heart-shaped taro leaves have always been the most common cooked greens in Hawaiian cooking, and this update on some luau classics shows their versatility. Here they are used as the basis for a rich sauce, a lumpia filling, and for wrapping foods for steaming. Although there really is no substitute for the earthy flavor of taro leaves, spinach or chard will give acceptable, if milder, results. My version of pipikaula—cured dried beef—is not dense or dry, but moist like pastrami or corned beef, which make the best substitutes in this recipe. Salted salmon is available at most fish markets, but you can prepare your own by rubbing an 8-ounce salmon fillet with $1/2$ cup kosher salt and allowing it to cure in the refrigerator for 24 to 48 hours.

TARO LEAF SAUCE

$1^1/2$ pounds fresh taro leaves

$1^1/2$ cups Veal Jus (page 179)

6 tablespoons Chicken Stock (page 177)

Salt and pepper to taste

LOMI SALMON

$1/4$ cup Lomi Tomato Relish (page 21)

1 tablespoon diced salted salmon

4 (7- to 8-ounce) boneless chicken breasts

Salt and pepper to taste

LUAU LUMPIA

4 lumpia wrappers

$1/4$ cup Kalua Pig (page 4)

2 ounces butterfish or rinsed salt cod, thinly sliced

1 egg, beaten

Vegetable oil for deep-frying

2 ounces warm Pipikaula (page 16) or pastrami or corned beef, cut into 8 slices

2 tablespoons Poi Vinaigrette (page 8)

2 tablespoons Tomato–Chile Pepper Vinaigrette (page 58)

4 sprigs thyme

To prepare the Taro Leaf Sauce, place the taro leaves in a steamer or vegetable basket set inside a saucepan of lightly boiling water. Cover and steam for 2 hours; there should be about 1 cup of steamed leaves. Set aside $1/4$ cup of the leaves.

In a saucepan, bring the remaining $3/4$ cup taro leaves, jus, and stock to a boil. Transfer to a blender and purée. Season with salt and pepper. Reheat before serving.

Prepare the grill.

To prepare the Lomi Salmon, in a bowl, combine the tomatoes and salmon. Refrigerate until needed.

Season the chicken with salt and pepper. Grill for 5 or 6 minutes on each side, or until cooked through.

To prepare the lumpias, lay a wrapper on a flat work surface, with a corner pointing toward you. Place 1 tablespoon of the reserved taro leaf in a horizontal line across the wrapper, corner to corner. Top with 1 tablespoon of the Kalua Pig and $3/4$ tablespoon of the butterfish. Fold the corner closest to you over the mixture, fold in the corners, and roll up tightly. Seal the edge with the whisked egg. Repeat for the remaining 3 lumpias.

In a deep fryer or large saucepan over high, heat about 3 inches of the vegetable oil to 375°. Deep-fry the lumpias for 2 to 3 minutes, or until golden and crispy. Remove and drain on paper towels. Halve each lumpia diagonally.

To serve, ladle about $1/2$ cup of the sauce onto individual plates. Slice each chicken breast and fan out in the center of the plate. Top each with the pipikaula and Lomi Salmon. Stand the lumpia halves upright next to the chicken with the diagonal cuts facing out. Drizzle both vinaigrettes over the Taro Leaf Sauce. Garnish the lumpias with a thyme sprig.

YIELD: 4 SERVINGS

If the salmon is very salty, soak in water and change the water—several times if necessary. Butterfish, or ling cod, is popular in Japanese cooking. It is typically used for the traditional Hawaiian Laulau (see page 20).

Pipikaula

Pipikaula—cured dried beef—is the local version of beef jerky that has been popular ever since cattle were introduced to the islands. One school of thought is that it was originally created by Hawaiians in the same style as the fish they had dried traditionally. Another suggests that it was introduced by the *paniolos*, or Mexican cowboys, who came to work on the cattle ranches and who brought their tradition of jerky with them.

3 quarts water

8 ounces salt

2 pinches curing salt

3 tablespoons sugar

2 bay leaves

1 tablespoon peppercorns

2 sprigs thyme

1/2 tablespoon cloves

1 pound flap meat or skirt steak, trimmed

Pepper to taste

In a stockpot, bring the water, salt, sugar, bay leaves, peppercorns, thyme, and cloves to a boil. Remove from the heat and let cool. Chill the curing brine in the refrigerator. Add the meat and marinate in the refrigerator for 24 hours.

Preheat the oven to 500°.

Remove the meat, pat dry, and season liberally with pepper. Place in a roasting pan and roast for 30 minutes, or until well done. Alternatively, grill the meat for 10 minutes on each side and then roast for 15 minutes.

YIELD: ABOUT 1 POUND

At the restaurant, our beef is supplied by Rick Habein of Kamuela Pride Ranch. Rick does indeed take great pride in raising humanely treated grass-fed cattle. He cares about his animals and the product he supplies, which is the reason they are not raised on hormones or antibiotics. In addition to caring about his animals, Rich also shares my passion for excellence—I like that.

Gingered Sweet Potatoes

The purple Okinawan sweet potatoes make a bold and unusual statement no matter how they are served. Their unusual color is an effective icebreaker at dinner parties. In this recipe, their flavor also provides a talking point as the Coconut-Ginger Cream gives them a taste rather like fortune cookies.

1 pound Okinawan (purple) sweet potatoes or regular sweet potatoes, peeled and chopped

3/4 cup warm Coconut-Ginger Cream (page 119)

Salt to taste

Place the potatoes in a steamer or a vegetable basket set in a saucepan of lightly boiling water. Cover and steam for 30 to 40 minutes, or until tender. Drain, transfer to a bowl, and mash. Add the Coconut-Ginger Cream and whisk until smooth. Season with salt.

YIELD: 4 SERVINGS

Lawalu Ehu: Leaf-Steamed Snapper with Mushroom Sauce

The *ehu*, or short-tailed red snapper, is a mildly flavored white-fleshed fish that is closely related to the *onaga*, or long-tailed red snapper, which can be substituted in this recipe. Snapper is a great fish for steaming because of its delicate, flaky texture. Wrapping it in leaves preserves its moist and tender quality. The banana leaves serve a practical purpose in the cooking process and also make an attractive and unusual presentation on the plates. For notes on ja-chai, see page 185.

1/2 cup finely julienned pork loin

2 1/2 tablespoons finely julienned ja-chai (Chinese pickled cabbage)

2 tablespoons peanut oil

1 1/2 tablespoons cornstarch

1 1/2 tablespoons Xao Xing Chinese cooking wine or dry cooking sherry

1 1/2 tablespoons Yamasa soy sauce or other brand

1 tablespoon oyster sauce

4 (6-ounce) ehu fillets

Salt and pepper to taste

4 square banana leaves or ti leaves

MUSHROOM SAUCE

1 teaspoon vegetable oil

1 teaspoon minced ginger

1/2 teaspoon minced garlic

1 1/2 cups Chicken Stock (page 177)

1 tablespoon oyster sauce

1/4 teaspoon dark sesame oil

1/4 teaspoon white vinegar

1/2 tablespoon cornstarch

1/2 tablespoon water

1 egg, beaten

1/2 cup thinly sliced shiitake mushrooms

1/2 tablespoon enoki mushrooms, cut into 1-inch lengths

1 tablespoon thinly sliced scallion, green part only

Salt and pepper to taste

Prepare the grill.

In a bowl, combine the pork, ja-chai, peanut oil, cornstarch, wine or sherry, soy sauce, and oyster sauce.

Season the ehu with salt and pepper. Lay a banana leaf on a flat work surface. Place a fillet in the center of the leaf. Spread the pork mixture over the fish, fold over the leaf to form a package, and secure with kitchen twine. Repeat for the remaining 3 packages.

Lawalu, wrapping fish or meat in ti or bananas leaves and steaming over hot coals, is another cooking technique typical of ancient Hawaii. This was done in a fire, rather than in the underground *imu* oven. The savory aromas of the cooking leaves and food was enjoyed as part of the process. *Lawalu* was a cooking method particularly favored by the *aliʻi,* or royalty.

Grill the packages over medium heat for 6 to 8 minutes, or until cooked through.

To prepare the sauce, in a saucepan over medium-high heat, heat the vegetable oil. Add the ginger and garlic and sauté for 2 minutes. Add the stock, oyster sauce, sesame oil, and vinegar and bring to a boil. Mix the cornstarch and water in a cup and stir into the saucepan. While stirring, add the beaten egg in a thin stream. Add the mushrooms and scallion and cook for 1 minute longer. Season with salt and pepper.

Place the packages on individual plates. Cut open at the table. Accompany with the sauce.

YIELD: 4 SERVINGS

Nori-Wrapped Akule Stuffed with Poke, and Wasabi Sauce

This recipe is a variation on the nori-wrapped ahi dish on page 53. Akule is a local type of scad mackerel that is a popular fish for pan-frying at home—my mom used to cook it often—but it rarely makes it onto restaurant menus. Stuffing fish with poke is an unusual presentation, but poke is a luau favorite. Here it is combined with a mouth-tingling take on the elegant, classic beurre blanc sauce. If you prefer, use 8 akule fillets rather than the whole fish.

4 sheets nori

4 akule, heads removed, cleaned, halved with the tail attached, and bones removed

1 1/2 cups Ahi Poke (page 54)

1 egg, beaten

Vegetable oil for deep-frying

1 cup all-purpose flour

3 cups Tempura Batter (page 53)

WASABI SAUCE

2 tablespoons wasabi powder

4 tablespoons hot water

2 tablespoons Yamasa soy sauce or other brand

1 cup Beurre Blanc (page 182)

1 teaspoon black sesame seeds

2 cups finely julienned daikon

40 to 48 stems enoki mushroom, trimmed

1/4 cup daikon or kaiware sprouts (optional)

1 tablespoon pickled ginger

4 chiso leaves

Place a sheet of nori on a flat work surface. Stuff the akule with the poke. Place a stuffed fish on the edge of the nori. Roll up the stuffed akule on the nori sheet (leaving the tail sticking out of one end). Trim the nori and seal the edge with the beaten egg. Alternatively, if using fillets, place 1 fillet on the nori, place a layer of poke on top, cover with a second fillet, roll, and seal. Repeat for the remaining 3 fish.

In a deep fryer or large saucepan, heat about 3 inches of vegetable oil to 350°. Dredge the nori-wrapped akule in the flour and then dip in the batter. Deep-fry the akule for 4 to 5 minutes, or until golden and crisp on the outside. Remove and drain on paper towels.

To prepare the wasabi sauce, in a bowl, whisk together the water and wasabi to form a smooth paste. Slowly stir in the soy sauce until thoroughly combined. Slowly add the wasabi mixture to the Beurre Blanc and stir until thoroughly incorporated. Keep warm.

To serve, cut the head-end half of each fish into 1/4-inch-thick slices and fan out onto individual plates. Stand the tail half of the fish upright on the plate next to the slices. Alternatively, if using fillets, slice and fan out the entire fish. Drizzle about 1/4 cup of the sauce around the akule and sprinkle with the sesame seeds. Place the daikon in a mound next to the akule and top with the enoki mushrooms and sprouts. Place the pickled ginger and chiso leaves next to the akule.

YIELD: 4 SERVINGS

Useful Hawaiian vocabulary for your next luau:

'ai a ma'ona: To eat as much as you like.

'ai iho: To eat.

aikane: Friend.

'aina: Meal.

aloha: Welcome, good-bye, love, affection.

haupa: To eat heartily.

hoa'ai: Eating companion.

keiki: Child.

lilio: Well fed; plump.

mahalo: Thank you.

mea'ai: Food.

okole maluna: A toast, roughly translated as "Bottoms up!"

ono: Delicious.

polili: Hungry.

Steamed Uku Laulau with Ginger-Scallion Sauce

Laulau is the traditional Hawaiian method of wrapping salted fish in taro and ti leaves and then steaming it in the *imu*. Later, the method was used for salted pork. In this recipe, we get much the same effect using ti leaves in a steamer. Like other snappers, the delicate flesh of the uku is best steamed. The Chinese-style sauce gives the perfect finishing touch without overwhelming the subtle flavors of the fish.

8 ti leaves or banana leaf squares

4 (6-ounce) uku (gray snapper) fillets

Salt to taste

4 ounces ogo (seaweed)

4 (1-ounce) slices lop cheong (Chinese sausage) or other hard sausage

GINGER-SCALLION SAUCE

¹/₄ cup finely julienned ginger

¹/₄ cup finely julienned scallions, white parts only

¹/₄ cup julienned onion

¹/₄ cup peanut oil

¹/₄ cup dark sesame oil

¹/₂ cup Chicken Stock (page 177)

¹/₄ cup Yamasa soy sauce or other brand

1 tablespoon cilantro leaves

Place 2 ti or banana leaves in a crisscross pattern on a flat work surface. Season the uku with salt. Place 1 fillet in the center of the leaves. Top the fish with one quarter of the ogo and a slice of the lop cheong. Fold over the ti leaves to form a package and secure with kitchen twine. Repeat for the remaining 3 packages.

Place the laulau packages in a steamer or vegetable basket set in a saucepan of lightly boiling water. Cover and steam for 8 to 10 minutes, or until cooked through.

To prepare the sauce, in a bowl, combine the ginger, scallions, and onion. Season with salt. Let sit for 3 minutes. In a saucepan over high heat, heat the peanut oil until just smoking. Carefully add to the bowl. Add the sesame oil, stock, and soy sauce and mix thoroughly.

To serve, place the packages on individual plates. Cut open at the table. Top the fish with the sauce.

YIELD: 4 SERVINGS

One of Hawaii's current sports heroes is Chad Rowan, a *yokozuna*, or sumo champion. Known in Japan as Akebono, Rowan was born and raised in Waimanalo, on the windward coast of Oahu. Recently interviewed by a local newspaper, the 6-foot-8-inch giant was asked if he is afraid of anyone. "Yeah," he replied, "my mom." And what did he miss most about home? "Da food. Poi, lomi salmon, kalua pig, and my mom's Franco-American Spaghetti." Well, spaghetti may not be on many luau menus, but if the other luau dishes are fine with Chad Rowan, who are we to argue?

Refried Taro

The taste and texture of Refried Taro is similar to refried pinto or black beans. I like to serve this side dish with Asian-style tacos, quesadillas, nachos, and other recipes with roots in Mexican and Southwestern cuisines.

2 tablespoons butter, at room
    temperature
Taro Smash (page 135)

In a sauté pan or skillet over medium-low heat, melt the butter. Increase the heat to medium-high. Add the Taro Smash and, stirring constantly, cook for 4 to 5 minutes, or until crispy.

YIELD: 4 TO 5 CUPS

Taro is a corm with edible leaves that has been the staff of life for Hawaiians since ancient times. Taro probably originated in the Malaysian peninsula. It had long been a daily staple for most societies in Polynesia before it was brought by the first settlers to Hawaii. There are over two hundred varieties worldwide and around fifty grown in Hawaii. While I find it hard to imagine that any place on earth consumes more than Hawaii, China uses the most taro in the world. Here's an interesting fact about taro: after it's harvested, the stalk and leaf growing from the top of the corm is cut and replanted by farmers. This natural recycling can also be done with pineapple tops and the root ends of garlic and onions.

Lomi Tomato Relish

Lomi is the Hawaiian word meaning "to crush, knead, or massage." The most famous *lomi* dish is lomi salmon, a luau standby (page 15), which actually is a relatively modern addition as salmon is not native to Hawaii. Salmon, together with salted cod, was introduced to the islands in the 1820s by missionaries and whalers from the U.S. East Coast.

This is an all-purpose relish that's like the traditional lomi salmon—only without the salmon! I like to use this relish as a topping to a number of dishes because the mild acidity of the tomatoes and onions livens up all kinds of other flavors. This simple relish is best used fresh, but it will keep in the refrigerator for up to 2 days.

1 cup diced vine-ripened tomato
$^1/_2$ cup finely diced sweet Maui onion
$^1/_4$ cup finely sliced scallions, green
    parts only
Salt to taste
Chile Pepper Water (page 175) to taste
    (optional)

In a small bowl, combine the tomato, onion, and scallions. Season with salt. Add the water to achieve the desired texture. Refrigerate until needed.

YIELD: $1^3/_4$ CUPS

Pūpū and Other Starters

Pūpū and Other Starters

I love the Hawaiian finger foods called *pūpū* as well as other starters. Small-portion appetizers with lots of flavors are my idea of fun eating. In many restaurants over the last few years, the concept of grazing, sampling several starters rather than ordering in the traditional way, has become the favored way of dining. Of course, it's nothing new: family-style Chinese cuisine is all about different flavors and textures, and the tradition of dim sum has long been popular in Chinese restaurants in the United States. Growing up, my mother would make family meals the same way. She would vary the dishes, but there would usually be something salty, something sweet, a sweet-and-sour dish, a spicy dish, and plain rice. She still likes to serve foods cooked using different methods, such as steamed, fried, and grilled on the same table. I'm sure this formative experience is why I still prefer to eat this way.

Because I like to create appetizers as much as I enjoy eating them, I am proud that many reviews have described them as a strength of the menu at Alan Wong's. We are always looking to tweak the recipes or change the presentation or flavor combinations, but we dare not alter our signature appetizers for fear of incurring the displeasure of our regular guests.

All of the recipes in this chapter are foods that I like to eat. Most Asian cuisines—and many others from around the world—are represented here, just as they are in Hawaii's melting pot. These soups, tacos, lumpias, quesadillas, salsas, and even foie gras are dishes that I created to incorporate local ingredients and flavors. With the distinctly Hawaiian manapua, ahi sashimi, and lomi tomatoes; the Korean kalbi; the Chinese li hing mui and wonton; the Japanese namasu; and the French-style aioli and lobster mousse, the recipes in this chapter have a little something for just about everyone.

Taro–Kalua Pig Chowder with Lomi Tomato Relish

Taro and Kalua pig are essential dishes found at authentic Hawaiian luaus, as described in detail on pages 2–3. The chunks of taro in the smooth soup give it a chowderlike consistency, but if you prefer, you can blend the taro with the soup and chill it overnight for a great taro vichyssoise.

4 cups cubed taro

1 tablespoon vegetable oil

2 cups diced onion

2 cups diced celery

2 cups diced leek, white parts only

2 tablespoons minced garlic

Salt to taste

8 cups Chicken Stock (page 177)

2 cups cubed potato

1/2 cup heavy cream

1 cup Kalua Pig (page 4) or shredded smoked or roast pork

1 cup Lomi Tomato Relish (page 21)

2 tablespoons Slivered Scallions (page 175), for garnish

In a vegetable basket set inside a saucepan of boiling water, steam 1 cup of the taro for 30 minutes, or until tender.

Meanwhile, in a large saucepan over medium-high heat, heat the vegetable oil. Sauté the onion, celery, and leek for 2 minutes, or until the onion is translucent. Add the garlic, salt, and stock and bring to a boil. Add the remaining 3 cups taro and the potato, reduce the heat to a simmer, and cook for about 20 minutes, or until the taro is tender.

Transfer the soup to a blender and purée until smooth. Place in a clean saucepan over low heat and stir in the cream. Cook, stirring occasionally, until the chowder is hot.

To serve, ladle into individual bowls and add the steamed taro. Top with the shredded pork, relish, and scallions.

YIELD: 4 SERVINGS

Hawaiian Koa Wood Bowls

Bowls made of wood, gourd, and fiber, known as calabashes, are an esteemed and beloved Hawaiian craft form. Traditionally used as containers for the poi served at luaus, wooden bowls such as those pictured throughout this book were particularly favored as royal gifts and heirlooms. Although calabashes were originally made from the wood of the revered kou tree, artisans began using another native wood, koa, as kou became increasingly scarce. Favored for their fine grain and satin sheen, koa wood bowls continue to embody the simple elegance that lies at the heart of Hawaii's rich cultural history.

Star Anise–Flavored Roast Duck and Cake Noodle Soup

Noodle soups are my favorites—I eat them almost every day. This is the perfect soup to make the day after enjoying roast duck—it's certainly the best way I know of using the duck carcass. Enjoy any leftover duck meat in spring rolls, risotto, or salad. If you live in a city with a Chinatown, or have a Chinese restaurant nearby, buy a Chinese roast duck and use that. This recipe is influenced strongly by Chinese flavors and ingredients, and it also shows my fondness for Vietnamese cuisine, especially *pho* (pronounced "fa"), a popular Hanoi noodle soup.

1 cooked duck carcass, quartered

8 cups Chicken Stock (page 177)

1 1/3 cups chopped whole scallions

2 shiitake mushrooms, quartered

1 (3-inch) piece of ginger, crushed

4 cloves garlic, halved

4 star anise

1 cinnamon stick

1 teaspoon fennel seeds

1 teaspoon coriander seeds

1 teaspoon cloves

1 teaspoon salt

CAKE NOODLES

1 cup fresh saimin noodles or cooked dried Chinese egg noodles

6 tablespoons vegetable oil

3/4 cup choy sum, spinach, or Chinese mustard cabbage (kai choy), for garnish

In a stockpot, bring the duck carcass, stock, scallions, mushrooms, ginger, garlic, star anise, cinnamon, fennel, coriander, cloves, and salt to a boil. Reduce the heat to low and simmer for 1 hour. Keep the heat low or the broth will taste bitter and become cloudy. Strain the broth and set aside.

To prepare the cake noodles, bring a saucepan of water to a boil and add the noodles. Cook for about 1 1/2 minutes, or until al dente. Drain and divide into 6 portions. In a nonstick sauté pan over high heat, heat 1 tablespoon of the oil. When hot, fry one noodle portion, shaking the pan gently in a circular motion so the noodles develop a nice round edge, for 4 to 5 minutes on each side, or until the noodles are crispy and golden. Keep warm.

Meanwhile, bring a saucepan of water to a boil. Blanch the choy sum for 30 seconds (or 5 seconds for spinach or 15 seconds for Chinese mustard cabbage) and transfer to an ice bath to stop it cooking further. Drain.

To serve, reheat the broth and pour into individual bowls. Place the noodles in the center of the broth. Garnish with the blanched choy sum and serve immediately.

YIELD: 6 SERVINGS

Chilled Tomato Soups with a Grilled Cheese and Kalua Pig Sandwich…and Foie Gras, of Course!

The yin-yang presentation remains one of my favorite ways of serving the soup portion of the recipe. The idea goes back to my days working on the East Coast, when I looked forward to eating grilled cheese sandwiches with hot tomato soup on chilly days. You don't get many chilly days in Honolulu, but I like to make this combination when special friends come to dine at my restaurant. There is a touch of unexpected decadence here, in the form of the foie gras. Alternative fillings that I enjoy include seared ahi, Pipikaula (page 16), truffles, and lobster with bacon.

SOUPS

2 ripe yellow tomatoes
    (about 4 ounces each)
2 ripe red tomatoes
    (about 4 ounces each)
2 teaspoons Chile Pepper Water
    (page 175)
2 teaspoons minced garlic
Salt to taste
1/4 cup olive oil

SANDWICHES

4 ounces foie gras
Salt and pepper to taste
1 teaspoon vegetable oil
2 tablespoons butter
8 slices French baguette, about
    1/4 inch thick
4 slices Fontina or mozzarella cheese,
    about 1/16 inch thick
4 tablespoons Kalua Pig (page 4), or
    shredded smoked or roasted pork
    (optional)

4 triangular sections of lavosh or
    poppadom, for garnish (optional)

Preheat the oven to 300°.

Place the tomatoes on a baking sheet and roast for 10 minutes. Remove from the oven and coarsely chop the tomatoes, keeping the colors separate.

To make the yellow soup, in a blender combine the yellow tomatoes and 1 teaspoon each of the Chile Pepper Water and garlic. Season with salt and purée until smooth. With the blender running, add half of the oil and blend until incorporated. Transfer to a small pitcher with a lip so it can be poured easily, and chill.

To make the red soup, in a blender combine the red tomatoes and the remaining Chile Pepper Water and garlic. Season with salt and purée until smooth. With the blender running, add the remaining oil and blend until incorporated. Transfer to a second small pitcher with a lip, and chill.

To serve, from opposite sides, simultaneously pour both soups into individual wine glasses to form a half-and-half or yin-and-yang pattern.

To prepare the sandwiches, using a warm knife, cut the foie gras into 4 slices about 1/4 inch thick and season with salt and pepper. In a small sauté pan over high heat, heat the vegetable oil. When the pan is very hot

and the oil begins to smoke, sear the foie gras for about 10 seconds on each side, or until golden brown. Let cool slightly.

Butter the bread slices on one side and place half the slices, buttered side down, on a work surface. Place a slice of cheese on the unbuttered side of each sandwich and top with the pork and a slice of foie gras. Close each sandwich with a bread slice, buttered side up.

In a sauté pan over medium-low heat, cook each sandwich for about 1 minute on each side, or until the cheese has melted and the bread has turned golden brown.

To serve, slice each sandwich in half and serve on a small plate to the side of each soup glass. Alternatively, place the triangular piece of lavosh or poppadom on top of the soup glass and balance the sandwich on top.

YIELD: 4 SERVINGS

Oxtail Soup with Wontons and Ginger-Soy Dipping Sauce

This is both a rich, delicious soup and medicine for the body and soul. Although oxtail soup is a traditional local comfort food, I didn't exactly take to it as a child. I think I just disliked the idea of eating a fly swatter! Luckily, I got over that prejudice and now often crave the reviving qualities of oxtail soup. This refined version has a distinctly Asian twist, with the addition of peanuts, ginger, soy, cilantro, star anise, wonton, and dried tangerine peel, which is available in Chinese markets and gives this soup an unexpected tanginess.

5 pounds oxtails

1 gallon water

6 scallions, white parts only

1 onion, chopped

1 head garlic, halved crosswise

1 (4-inch) piece of ginger, crushed

3 pieces dried tangerine peel

4 star anise

Salt to taste

24 raw shelled peanuts

GINGER-SOY
DIPPING SAUCE

5 tablespoons Yamasa soy sauce
   or other brand

2 tablespoons minced ginger

1 tablespoon Chile Pepper Water
   (page 175)

1 tablespoon chopped cilantro

WONTONS

18 square wonton wrappers or
   thin ravioli wrappers

1 egg, whisked

2 shiitake mushrooms, sliced

1 tablespoon minced cilantro

2 tablespoons sliced scallions,
   green parts only

2 tablespoons julienned Chinese
   mustard cabbage (kai choy)

Cut the oxtail into segments by feeling where each vertebra lies and slicing slightly behind each notch so that you are slicing through the cartilage and not the bone.

In a stockpot, bring the oxtails, water, scallions, onion, garlic, ginger, tangerine peel, star anise, and salt to a boil. Reduce the heat and simmer, covered, for about 3 hours, or until the oxtail meat easily falls away from the bones. Add the peanuts after 2 hours. Do not overcook, or the soup will taste bitter and become cloudy. Skim the surface of the soup occasionally to remove any impurities that rise to the surface. Strain the broth, reserving the liquid. When cool, remove the meat from the bones and set aside. Remove the peanuts and set aside.

To make the dipping sauce, in a small bowl, whisk together the soy sauce, ginger, Chile Pepper Water, and chopped cilantro. Pour into 6 small ramekins and set aside.

To prepare the wontons, place 1 tablespoon of the reserved oxtail meat on one side of each wrapper. Lightly brush the edge of the wrapper with the whisked egg and fold the wrapper over diagonally, enclosing the meat to form a triangle. Press the edges of the wrapper to seal. Fold in the 2 corners furthest apart, add a little whisked egg, and press them together to seal. Bring a saucepan of water to a boil. Add the wontons and cook for about 1 minute, or until the wontons lose their cornstarch taste.

To serve, place 3 wontons in individual bowls and pour in the hot broth. Top with the reserved cooked peanuts, shiitakes, cilantro, scallions, and cabbage. Serve with the dipping sauce, which should be used for the wontons.

YIELD: 6 SERVINGS

Crab Cakes on Ginger-Scallion Aioli with Cucumber-Carrot Namasu

One day, I happened to have an abundance of Lobster Mousse on hand—more than I needed for the California Rolls (page 32)—so I began experimenting with it as a binding for crabcakes. The results were spectacular, and the appetizer has remained on my menu ever since. Namasu is a Japanese condiment, typical of Hawaiian bento box lunches.

CUCUMBER-CARROT NAMASU

1 cup rice wine vinegar

1/2 cup sugar

1 (1-inch) piece of ginger, julienned

2/3 cup thinly angle-sliced Japanese cucumber or seeded hothouse cucumber

1/3 cup thinly angle-sliced carrots

GINGER-SCALLION AIOLI

1 cup Aioli (page 182)

1 tablespoon Ginger-Scallion Oil (page 180)

1 cup loosely packed spinach

LOBSTER MOUSSE

1 teaspoon butter

1 shallot, minced

4 fresh uncooked lobster tails (about 4 ounces each), shelled and chopped

1 egg white

Salt to taste

1 1/4 cups heavy cream

CRAB CAKES

1 tablespoon vegetable oil plus more for deep-frying

1 cup finely diced celery

1 cup finely diced onion

2 cups loosely packed chopped fresh flat-leaf parsley

2 cups fresh crabmeat

1 cup flour

2 eggs

1/2 cup milk

4 cups panko or bread crumbs

To prepare the namasu, in a bowl, combine the vinegar, sugar, and ginger and stir until the sugar dissolves. Add the cucumber and carrots and marinate in the refrigerator for at least 2 hours, or overnight.

To prepare the aioli, in a blender, combine the plain aioli, oil, and spinach and purée until smooth. Refrigerate until needed.

To prepare the mousse, in a small sauté pan over medium heat, melt the butter. Add the shallot and sweat for about 45 seconds, or until translucent. Let cool and transfer to a food processor. Add the lobster, egg white, and salt and purée until smooth. With the machine running, slowly add the cream in a steady stream until fully incorporated; do not overmix. Refrigerate until needed.

To prepare the crab cakes, in a sauté pan over medium-high heat, heat 1 tablespoon of the vegetable oil. Add the celery and onion and sauté for 2 minutes, or until the onion is translucent. Chill. Transfer to a bowl, add the mousse, parsley, and crab meat and mix well. Divide the mixture into 8 portions and form into balls.

Place the flour on a plate. Roll the balls in the flour until lightly coated. In a bowl, whisk together the eggs and milk. Place the panko in a large plate. Dunk the crab cake balls in the egg mixture and then roll in the panko to cover. Repeat the egg and panko steps. Place a 2-inch cookie cutter on a work surface and form each ball into the round shape of the cookie cutter. Refrigerate for at least 10 minutes.

In a deep fryer or large saucepan, heat about 3 inches of vegetable oil to 350°. Add the crab cakes and deep-fry for about 1 minute, or until they rise to the surface of the oil and turn golden brown. Flip over and cook for 1 minute, or until golden brown.

To serve, divide the aioli among individual plates. Place 2 crab cakes on top of the aioli. Using a slotted spoon, remove the cucumber, carrot, and ginger from the marinade and serve next to the crab cakes.

YIELD: 4 SERVINGS

Hot California Rolls with
Kona Lobster Mousse...but with No Rice!

Traditionally, Asian-style California rolls are made with rice, crab, and avocado wrapped inside a sheet of nori. This version replaces the rice with a traditional French-style lobster mousse—another successful example of East meeting West. One other departure here is that these rolls are served hot. You might want to prepare the Aioli (page 182) first as it is used both in the mousse and as the base for the Chile Pepper Aioli that is used as a garnish. Store the excess dressing in the refrigerator for up to 1 week; shake well before using. (*Note: Recipes containing raw eggs are not recommended for immuno-compromised individuals or small children.*)

SOY MUSTARD

1 1/2 tablespoons mustard powder

1 1/2 tablespoons warm water

1 tablespoon Yamasa soy sauce
   or other brand

Lobster Mousse (page 31)

2 tablespoons Aioli (page 182)

1 tablespoon Chile Pepper Aioli
   (page 183)

2 ounces cooked Dungeness crabmeat
   (about 1/2 cup)

1 teaspoon cayenne

1 teaspoon freshly squeezed
   lemon juice

1/2 cup fresh corn kernels (from
   1 ear corn)

1/2 avocado, diced

3 sheets nori (8 inches square)

TARRAGON VINAIGRETTE

1 egg

1 tablespoon Dijon mustard

1/4 cup plus 2 tablespoons tarragon
   vinegar

2 teaspoons minced garlic

2 teaspoons minced shallots

2 cups olive oil

Salt to taste

Up to 1/4 cup water

1/4 cup tobiko

4 tablespoons salmon caviar,
   for garnish

4 tablespoons wasabi tobiko,
   for garnish

Mixed salad greens, for garnish

To prepare the soy mustard, in a bowl, mix the mustard powder with the water to form a smooth paste. Stir in the soy sauce. Set aside.

Prepare the Lobster Mousse, Aioli, and Chile Pepper Aioli and re-frigerate until needed.

In a mixing bowl, combine the crabmeat, plain aioli, cayenne, lemon juice, corn, and avocado.

Cut one nori sheet in half lengthwise and place on a work surface. Spread the crab mixture in a line across the long side and roll up. Place a full nori sheet on a work surface. Spread with an even layer of the mousse. Place the crab roll on top of the mousse and roll up. Repeat this process with the remaining half and full nori sheets. Wrap both rolls in plastic wrap and chill in the refrigerator for 15 minutes to firm the mixture and facilitate handling.

Preheat the oven to 350°.

Slice each roll into 6 pieces. Place a pearl-sized amount of the Chile Pepper Aioli at the top of each slice. Transfer the slices to a lightly oiled nonstick baking sheet and bake for 8 to 10 minutes, or until the mousse is cooked through.

To prepare the vinaigrette, in a blender, combine the egg, mustard, vinegar, garlic, and shallots and purée. With the machine running, add the olive oil and blend until incorporated. Season with salt. If the mixture becomes too stiff, add the water a little at a time until the desired consistency is reached; the vinaigrette should be pourable. Stir in the tobiko.

To serve, arrange 3 slices of the rolls on each plate and drizzle with the soy mustard. Pour the vinaigrette around each plate. Garnish with the salmon caviar, wasabi tobiko, and salad greens.

YIELD: 4 SERVINGS

Hoisin Baby Back Ribs

It's always gratifying to see serving plates of these mouthwatering ribs come back to the kitchen with just a hill of gnawed-down bones on them. The hoisin barbecue sauce has its origins in my attempt to recreate the flavors I remember so well from family hibachi barbecues I enjoyed in the backyard or at the beach as a child. When we removed this starter from the menu, our guests requested it anyway, so it became a regular item. This recipe is best prepared the day before cooking to allow the ribs to marinate overnight. The method of grilling the ribs before steaming them in the oven captures the wonderful, smoky flavor. The barbecue sauce is great for grilled chicken or pork. A fruity wine such as Zinfandel matches these ribs superbly.

SAUCE

$3/4$ cup hoisin sauce

1 cup ketchup

$1/2$ cup honey

5 tablespoons Yamasa soy sauce or other brand

5 tablespoons dry sherry

$1/4$ cup plus 2 tablespoons white wine vinegar

$1/4$ cup white sesame seeds, toasted

2 tablespoons plus 2 teaspoons curry powder

2 tablespoons plus 2 teaspoons dark sesame oil

2 tablespoons grated orange zest

2 tablespoons fermented black beans

2 tablespoons minced garlic

1 tablespoon minced red Hawaiian chiles or red serrano chiles with seeds, or 1 tablespoon chile sauce with garlic

3 pounds pork baby back ribs

Salt and pepper to taste

To prepare the sauce, in a mixing bowl, combine the hoisin sauce, ketchup, honey, soy sauce, sherry, vinegar, sesame seeds, curry, oil, orange zest, beans, garlic, and chiles and whisk until blended.

Divide the ribs among 2 large baking dishes and brush with half of the sauce. Cover the ribs and the remaining sauce separately, and refrigerate overnight.

Prepare the grill and preheat the oven to 375°.

Discard the marinade and season the ribs with salt and pepper. Grill for 15 minutes, turning frequently. Transfer the ribs to a roasting pan, add 1 inch of water, and cover with foil. Cook in the oven for about 2 hours, or until fork tender. Remove the ribs from the pan, let cool, and marinate them in half of the reserved sauce.

In a saucepan over medium-high heat, bring the remaining sauce to a simmer.

To serve, reheat the ribs in the oven for about 10 to 15 minutes. Cut them into individual ribs and transfer to a serving platter. Pass the heated sauce separately.

YIELD: 6 SERVINGS

Manapua-Style Quesadillas with Fresh Water Chestnut–Tomato Salsa

I grew up on *manapua*, the Hawaiian-Chinese steamed bun filled with char siu bao, or shredded barbecue pork. Here, I adapted that flavor to the quesadilla concept, creating an unlikely Chinese-Hawaiian-Mexican hybrid you'll want to try to believe it works. Fresh water chestnuts, available in Chinese markets, have a unique sweetness and crunch, but you can substitute jicama. You need to marinate the meat a day before preparing the quesadillas.

MARINADE

2 1/2 tablespoons sugar

1 tablespoon hoisin sauce

2 tablespoons fermented bean curd or soybean paste

2 tablespoons sherry

3 drops red food coloring (optional)

1/2 teaspoon Chinese five-spice powder

Pinch of minced garlic

Pinch of minced ginger

Salt to taste

1 pound boneless pork butt, cut into strips 6 inches long and 1 inch wide

3 tablespoons minced onion

1/2 tablespoon minced garlic

3 tablespoons sliced scallion, green and white parts

3 tablespoons hoisin sauce

3 tablespoons chile sauce with garlic

2 teaspoons Chile Pepper Water (page 175)

8 (6-inch) flour tortillas

8 ounces mozzarella cheese, cut into 8 thin slices

32 cilantro leaves (optional)

1 cup Fresh Water Chestnut Salsa (page 131)

2 tablespoons Slivered Scallion (page 175), for garnish

1/2 tablespoon Asian Oil (page 180)

1/2 tablespoon Chile Oil (page 180)

To prepare the marinade, in a large bowl, combine the sugar, hoisin sauce, bean curd or soybean paste, sherry, food coloring, five-spice powder, garlic, and ginger. Season with salt. Add the pork, cover, and marinate in the refrigerator for at least 24 hours.

Preheat the oven to 350°. Line a roasting pan with aluminum foil, pour 1 to 2 inches of hot water in the pan, and place a wire rack in the bottom of the pan.

Remove the meat from the marinade and arrange on the rack in a single layer. Cover with foil and roast for 1 hour, turning the meat after 30 minutes.

Dice one eighth of the meat and reserve. Coarsely chop the remaining pork, place in the bowl of a food processor, and process into a hashlike consistency. Transfer to a mixing bowl and add the reserved diced meat, onion, garlic, scallion, hoisin sauce, chile sauce, and Chile Pepper Water. Combine well and refrigerate until needed.

On a work surface, lay out 4 of the tortillas. On each, place a slice of cheese, 2 heaping tablespoons of the pork mixture, 8 cilantro leaves, and another piece of cheese. Top with the remaining tortillas.

Working in batches in a dry sauté pan over medium-low heat, cook the quesadillas for 5 minutes—3 minutes on one side and 2 minutes on the other—or until the cheese has melted and the filling is hot, and the tortillas are lightly browned; be careful not to let them burn.

To serve, place 1/4 cup of the salsa in the center of individual plates. Cut each quesadilla into 8 wedges and arrange around the salsa. Garnish with the scallions. Lightly drizzle the Asian Oil and Chile Oil around each plate.

YIELD: 4 SERVINGS

Manapua is derived from three Hawaiian words, *mea ono pua*, and means "tasty food filled with pork"; it's typical fare in Hawaii's Chinatown and particularly popular as a dim sum item.

Curried Chicken Lumpia with
Mango Salsa and Sweet-and-Sour Sauce

"Mom," as my staff calls my mother, comes to cook in the restaurant kitchen most weekends. She's the only cook allowed to set her own schedule. This is her lumpia recipe, and it's the best one I've come across. Lumpia—a fried egg roll traditionally filled with pork, shrimp, and vegetables—is a classic Filipino dish enhanced here with flavors from India and the lush taste of local mango. You can substitute crab or lobster for the chicken.

MANGO VINAIGRETTE

1 mango, chopped

$1/2$ tablespoon freshly squeezed lime juice

Pinch of salt

2 teaspoons olive oil

SWEET-AND-SOUR SAUCE

$3/4$ cup ketchup

2 tablespoons peanut oil

2 tablespoons sherry

$1/4$ cup oyster sauce

6 tablespoons brown sugar

$1/4$ cup red wine vinegar

2 tablespoons sesame oil

1 teaspoon minced ginger

$1/2$ teaspoon minced garlic

$1/4$ teaspoon minced red Hawaiian chile or red serrano chile

Salt to taste

2 chicken thighs

2 bay leaves

1 teaspoon black peppercorns

2 teaspoons vegetable oil plus more for deep-frying

$1/2$ cup sliced shiitake mushrooms

4 snow peas, stringed

$1/4$ cup cooked Dungeness crabmeat

$1/2$ tablespoon curry powder

$1/2$ teaspoon Chile Pepper Water (page 175)

2 lumpia wrappers

$1/2$ teaspoon finely julienned ginger

1 egg, beaten

2 tablespoons hoisin sauce

1 sprig basil or amaranth, for garnish

Mango Salsa (page 128)

To prepare the vinaigrette, in a blender, combine the mango, lime juice, and salt and purée until smooth. With the machine running, slowly add the oil until incorporated. Refrigerate until needed.

To prepare the sweet-and-sour sauce, in a blender, combine the ketchup, peanut oil, sherry, oyster sauce, sugar, vinegar, sesame oil, ginger, garlic, chile, and salt and purée until smooth. Refrigerate until needed.

In a small pan of boiling water, place the chicken thighs, bay leaves, and peppercorns and boil for 45 minutes, or until cooked through. When cool, shred the chicken meat and set aside. Discard the bones, bay leaves, and peppercorns. In small sauté pan over medium-high heat, heat 2 teaspoons of the oil. When hot, sauté the mushrooms for 2 minutes. Blanch the snow peas in boiling water for 1 minute, drain, and transfer to an ice bath to cool.

In a mixing bowl, combine the shredded chicken, mushrooms, crabmeat, curry powder, and Chile Pepper Water. Place a lumpia wrapper on a work surface with a corner pointing toward you. Place $1/4$ cup of the filling in a horizontal line, across the wrapper, corner to corner. Place half of the ginger on top of the mixture and 1 snow pea on each side. Fold the corner closest to you over the mixture, fold in the corners, and roll up tightly. Seal the edge with the beaten egg. Repeat for the second lumpia.

In a deep fryer or large saucepan over high heat, heat about 3 inches of vegetable oil to 350°. Add the lumpias and deep-fry for about $1 1/2$ to 2 minutes, or until golden and crispy. Cut each lumpia in half diagonally.

To serve, place the vinaigrette, sweet-and-sour sauce, and hoisin sauce in separate squeeze bottles and drizzle 3 parallel zig-zag designs (using about 1 teaspoon of each sauce) on a serving dish. Alternatively, using a spoon, place dollops of each sauce artistically on the plate. Stand the lumpia halves upright on the plate, with the diagonal cut facing out. Garnish with a basil sprig. Accompany with the Mango Salsa.

YIELD: 4 SERVINGS

Island-Style Foie Gras with Pineapple and Li Hing Mui Chutney

Li hing mui, or sweet-sour marinated plums, is one of the popular kinds of crack seed, the popular Hawaiian preserved fruit snack. My chutney version of *li hing mui* is just sweet and sour enough to complement the rich foie gras, and the acid of the fruit perfectly balances its rich flavors, making a delicious combination.

PINEAPPLE VINAIGRETTE

1 1/2 cups diced sweet pineapple

1 1/2 tablespoons balsamic vinegar

2 tablespoons olive oil

Salt to taste

BALSAMIC RUM SYRUP

1/4 cup water

1/4 cup sugar

1/2 cup balsamic vinegar

1 teaspoon dark rum

8 very thin slices sweet pineapple

8 to 10 ounces foie gras,
    cut into 4 slices

Salt and pepper to taste

4 teaspoons Basil Oil (page 181)

Li Hing Mui Chutney (page 133)

To prepare the vinaigrette, in a blender, combine the pineapple and vinegar and purée until smooth. With the machine running, slowly add the olive oil until incorporated. Season with salt. Refrigerate until needed.

To prepare the Balsamic Rum Syrup, in a saucepan, bring the water and sugar to a boil. Boil until reduced by half. Add the balsamic vinegar, return to a boil, and boil until reduced by one third. Stir in the rum and refrigerate until needed.

Preheat the oven to 200°. Line a baking sheet with lightly oiled parchment paper.

Place 4 pineapple slices on the baking sheet and dry in the oven for about 8 hours or overnight.

Season the foie grass with salt and pepper. In a nonstick sauté pan over medium-high heat, sear the foie gras for about 2 minutes on each side, or until golden brown.

Arrange the remaining fresh pineapple slices in the center of individual plates. Using a squeeze bottle or spoon, carefully drizzle the Basil Oil around the edge of each pineapple slice. Place the seared foie gras on top of the pineapple. Drizzle the vinaigrette and syrup on the foie gras. Top with the chutney. Lean the oven-dried pineapple slices against the foie gras.

YIELD: 4 SERVINGS

Crack seed was brought to Hawaii in the nineteenth century by Cantonese Chinese immigrants. In the islands, it is an adult snack as well as a candy surrogate for children. Crack seed can be sweet, sour, sweet-and-sour, salty, very salty, anise-flavored, ginger-flavored, fruit-flavored, dry, or wet. All kinds of fruits, such as plums, apricots, mangoes, papayas, olives, lemons, guava, cherries, and even ginger are dried and flavored for this popular treat.

NEW WAVE TACO PLATE

The following three recipes make up what I call my "New Wave Taco Plate": a Mexican favorite given a distinctly Asian twist.

Seared Ahi Tuna Tacos

Here, wonton wrappers replace the traditional corn tortillas. If round wonton wrappers are unavailable, no problem! Using a round cookie cutter or kitchen scissors. trim the square wrappers into circles. If you plan on making any of these recipes more than once, consider buying a taco deep fryer, available in kitchen specialty stores. Try any of these tacos with Alan's Asian Guacamole (page 128).

2 tablespoons olive oil

8 ounces ahi tuna, cut into 2 pieces 6 inches long and 1/4 inch thick

2 tablespoons shichimi togorashi

Salt to taste

Vegetable oil for deep-frying

8 round wonton wrappers

16 sprigs mizuna lettuce (optional)

1 cup shredded lettuce

2 tablespoons pickled ginger

1 tablespoon Slivered Scallions (page 175)

2 cups Steamed White Rice (page 136)

4 pinches black sesame seeds, for garnish

In a sauté pan over high heat, heat the olive oil until hot but not smoking. Sprinkle both sides of the tuna with the shichimi and salt. Sear for about 8 seconds on each side, or until the exterior appears cooked but the interior is raw. When cool, cut each portion into 6 slices.

In a deep fryer or large saucepan over high heat, heat about 3 inches of vegetable oil to 350°. Using a pair of tongs in each hand, hold the opposite sides of each wonton wrapper to form a U and place in the hot oil. (If using one pair of tongs, hold one side of the wonton down with a spoon while folding the other side over with the tongs.) Fry for 3 to 4 minutes, or until golden and crisp. Remove and drain on paper towels.

To assemble the tacos, place 2 mizuna sprigs on the bottom of each wrapper, sticking outwards. Add the shredded lettuce, 3 slices of tuna, pickled ginger, and scallions. To serve, place 2 tacos on each individual plate. Serve with the rice garnished with the sesame seeds.

YIELD: 4 SERVINGS

Tamarind-Glazed Shrimp Tacos

Shrimp cooked with a tamarind glaze gives a tropical Southeast Asian feel to this taco. Tamarind is used for its intriguing, tart, flavorful qualities in Mexican and Asian cuisines, which makes it a particularly appropriate ingredient in these New Wave tacos. The refried taro in this recipe is a twist on the classic Mexican side dish of refried beans, and the texture and flavors are surprisingly similar.

$^1/_2$ **cup water**

$^1/_2$ **cup sugar**

$^1/_4$ **cup freshly squeezed lemon juice**

$^1/_4$ **cup plus 1 tablespoon tamarind paste**

2 tablespoons honey

1 tablespoon cayenne

$^1/_2$ **tablespoon ground cumin**

$^1/_2$ **tablespoon ground coriander**

$^1/_2$ **tablespoon fennel seed**

8 fresh jumbo shrimp (about 8 ounces), shelled and deveined

Vegetable oil for deep-frying

8 round wonton wrappers

2 cups Refried Taro (page 21)

1 cup Alan's Asian Guacamole (page 128)

1 cup julienned green cabbage, for garnish

Prepare the grill.

In a bowl, combine the water, sugar, lemon juice, tamarind paste, honey, cayenne, cumin, coriander, and fennel.

When the grill is hot, add the shrimp and cook for 2 minutes. Brush with the glaze, turn over, brush the other side, and continue to cook for another 2 minutes, or until pink and cooked through. Brush on more glaze just before removing the shrimp from the grill. Alternatively, in a sauté pan over medium-high heat, heat 1 tablespoon of vegetable oil. Sauté the shrimp for 3 minutes, or until pink and cooked through.

In a deep fryer or large saucepan over high heat, heat about 3 inches of vegetable oil to 350°. Using a pair of tongs in each hand, hold the opposite sides of each wonton wrapper to form a U and place in the hot oil. (If using one pair of tongs, hold one side of the wonton down with a spoon while folding the other side over with the tongs.) Fry for 3 to 4 minutes, or until golden and crisp. Remove and drain on paper towels.

To assemble the tacos, divide the taro among the wrappers. Add 2 tablespoons of the guacamole and a shrimp. To serve, divide the cabbage among individual plates. Arrange 2 tacos on top.

YIELD: 4 SERVINGS

Kalbi Short Rib Tacos
with Papaya–Red Onion Salsa

I really enjoy Korean food, especially those dishes that include my favorite ingredients: chiles, garlic, and sesame seeds. I'm also addicted to good Korean barbecue. The essential flavoring for kalbi—the Korean dish of barbecued short ribs—is the slightly sweet, slightly tart, slightly spicy, and plenty garlicky marinade replicated here. Kalbi is popular in Hawaii, and you can smell it in the air at picnics and from family hibachis at the beach.

2 cups Yamasa soy sauce or other brand

2 cups water

2 cups sugar

Juice of 4 lemons

4 kaffir lime leaves

1 head garlic, halved

2 red Hawaiian chiles, or 1 red serrano chile with seeds, smashed

$^1/_2$ cup sesame oil

4 tablespoons white sesame seeds, toasted

2 tablespoons Chile Pepper Water (page 175)

3 stalks lemongrass, chopped

2 tablespoons Thai red curry paste

1 cup chopped scallions, white parts only

8 ounces beef short ribs (about $^1/_4$ inch thick)

2 tablespoons cornstarch

Vegetable oil for deep-frying

8 round wonton wrappers

8 leaves butter lettuce

Papaya–Red Onion Salsa (page 130)

2 serrano chiles with seeds, thinly sliced, for garnish

16 cilantro sprigs, for garnish

In a large bowl, combine the soy sauce, water, sugar, lemon juice, lime leaves, garlic, chiles, sesame oil, 3 tablespoons of the sesame seeds, Chile Pepper Water, lemongrass, curry paste, and scallions. Remove and refrigerate $^3/_4$ cup of the marinade. Place the ribs in the bowl of marinade and marinate in the refrigerator for at least 24 hours.

Prepare the grill.

Remove the ribs from the marinade and bring to room temperature. Discard the rib marinade.

In a saucepan over medium-high heat, heat the reserved marinade. In a bowl, mix 2 tablespoons of the marinade with the cornstarch. Return the cornstarch mixture to the pan, stirring vigorously, and bring the sauce to a boil. Remove from the heat and set aside.

Grill the ribs for 6 to 8 minutes for medium-rare or 8 to 10 minutes for medium. Cut the meat from the ribs, dice, and add to the sauce.

In a deep fryer or large saucepan over high heat, heat about 3 inches of vegetable oil to 350°. Using a pair of tongs in each hand, hold the opposite sides of each wonton wrapper to form a U and place in the hot oil. (If using one pair of tongs, hold one side of the wonton down with a spoon while folding the other side over with the tongs.) Fry for 3 to 4 minutes, or until golden and crisp. Remove and drain on paper towels.

To assemble the tacos, place a butter lettuce leaf on the bottom of each wrapper, sticking outwards. Add the rib meat, sauce, and salsa. Garnish with the remaining sesame seeds, chiles, and cilantro.

To serve, divide among individual plates.

YIELD: 4 SERVINGS

The New Wave Taco Plate (from top): Tamarind-Glazed Shrimp Taco (page 41),
Kalbi Short Rib Taco with Papaya–Red Onion Salsa (this page), and
Seared Ahi Tuna Taco (page 40).

Sliced Chinese Roast Duck on
Tapioca Chips and Asian Guacamole

Most people associate tapioca with its pearllike form, but the yuca (or cassava) plant from which it comes is also ground into starch. One excellent use for tapioca flour is crepes. One day when I was experimenting with tapioca crepes in the kitchen at the Mauna Lani, instead of griddling the crepes, I decided to deep-fry them to see how they would turn out. The result was crisp, tasty chips, and from there I created this dish. Duck, hoisin, and scallions are matched in Chinese Peking Duck recipes; the whole dish is a true culinary fusion.

TAPIOCA CHIPS

7 1/2 ounces tapioca starch

1/4 cup all-purpose flour

1 1/4 cups hot tap water

1/2 cup half-and-half

1 egg

3/4 cup finely sliced scallions, green parts only

1 teaspoon cayenne

Salt to taste

3 teaspoons vegetable oil

TOMATO-GINGER COULIS

1/4 cup olive oil

1 clove garlic, sliced

1 (1/2-inch) piece of ginger, sliced

3/4 cup diced tomato

1/4 cup Chicken Stock (page 177)

Salt and pepper to taste

TARO CHIPS

Vegetable oil for deep-frying

20 very thin slices taro

SWEET POTATO CHIPS

Vegetable oil for deep-frying

12 very thin slices Okinawan purple sweet potato or regular sweet potato

LINGUINE STICKS

Vegetable oil for deep-frying

20 pieces dried linguine or spaghetti

1/2 cup Refried Taro (page 21)

1 cup Alan's Asian Guacamole (page 128)

5 to 6 ounces roast duck breast, cut into 20 thin slices

2 teaspoons hoisin sauce

Slivered Scallions (page 175), for garnish

To prepare the tapioca chips, in a stainless steel bowl, combine the tapioca, flour, water, half-and-half, and egg and whisk until all the lumps are gone. Add the scallions, cayenne, and salt. In a small nonstick pan over medium-low heat, heat the vegetable oil. Ladle 2 tablespoons of the batter into the hot pan, tilting the pan so the batter spreads evenly. Cook for 1 to 2 minutes on each side, or until brown spots mark the underside of the crepes. Remove the crepes and set aside. Repeat for 2 more crepes.

To prepare the coulis, in a saucepan over medium heat, heat the olive oil. Add the garlic and ginger and sauté until lightly brown. Add the tomatoes and stock and bring to a boil. Simmer, uncovered, for 20 to 25 minutes, or until the coulis is reduced to about 1/2 cup. Transfer to a blender and purée until smooth. Season with salt and pepper, strain into a bowl, and refrigerate until needed.

To prepare the Taro Chips, Sweet Potato Chips, and Linguine Sticks, in a deep fryer or large saucepan, heat about 3 inches of vegetable oil to 375°. Deep-fry the taro for 3 to 4 minutes, or until crisp and golden. Remove and drain on paper towels. Deep-fry the sweet potato for 3 to 4 minutes, or until crisp. Remove and drain on paper towels. Deep-fry the linguine for about 1 1/2 minutes, or until crisp. Remove and drain on paper towels. Cut each crepe into 8 triangles. Deep-fry these tapioca chips for 2 to 3 minutes, or until crisp and golden brown. Drain on paper towels.

To serve, divide the Refried Taro and guacamole among individual plates. Surround with the taro, sweet potato, and tapioca chips, and the pasta. Arrange 5 or 6 deep-fried tapioca chips evenly around the taro and guacamole and drizzle some of the coulis between each chip. Place 1 teaspoon of guacamole on each chip and top with a slice of duck breast. Place a pea-size dollop of hoisin sauce on each slice of duck and garnish with the slivered scallions.

YIELD: 4 SERVINGS

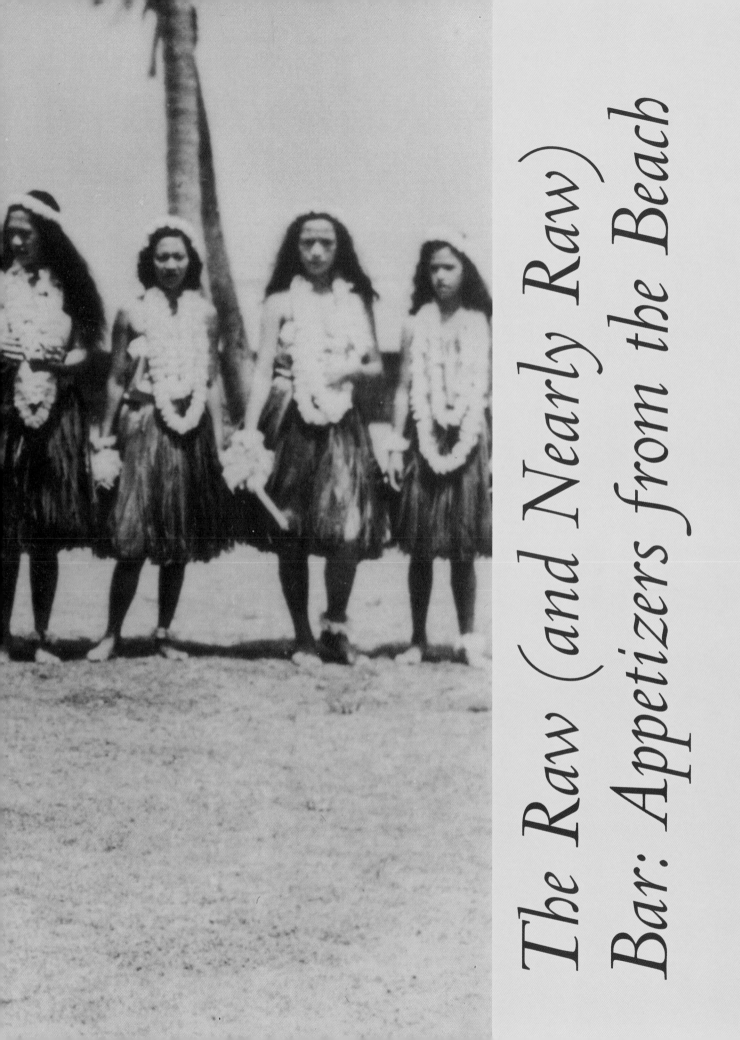

The Raw (and Nearly Raw)
Bar: Appetizers from the Beach

The Raw (and Nearly Raw) Bar: Appetizers from the Beach

The appetizers in this chapter have one thing in common: the sea. Since ancient times, the ocean has been an important source of food. The traditional luaus of the last century featured different types of poke; a'ama crab; opihi (limpets); limu, ogo, and other types of seaweed; seaweed salads; wana (sea urchin); and other foods from the Pacific waters around Hawaii.

Raw and rare-seared fresh fish and shellfish are well represented on our appetizer menu at Alan Wong's. I have always enjoyed eating sashimi, poke, and raw seafood: when you are born in Hawaii, you grow up on it. There is good, fresh fish and shellfish all across the islands, and there are few better places on earth than Hawaii if you love quality seafood.

Not only does the unadulterated taste of seafood please the palate, but these precious jewels of the ocean are also a wonderful source of nutrition. Fish and seafood are low in fat and cholesterol and high in certain vitamins, such as A, B6, B12, and D. They are also high in beneficial minerals such as calcium, potassium, phosphorous, iodine, and fluorine. The more oily fish such as salmon, tuna, and mackerel contain essential fatty acids that favorably affect blood cholesterol levels and help prevent heart disease.

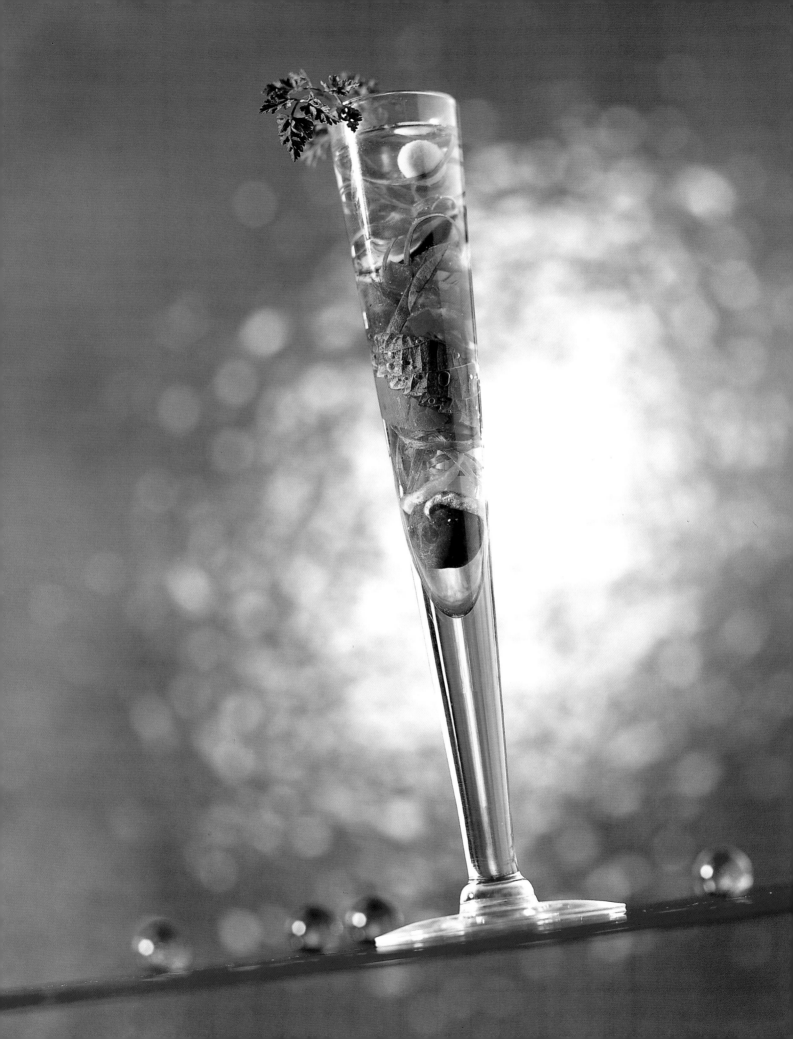

The New Wave Opihi Shooter

Opihi, a limpet native to Hawaii, is a prized shellfish that, in times gone by, was a popular delicacy enjoyed at luaus. It is found more rarely now, which makes it expensive—opihi cost up to $300 a gallon in shucked form. Another reason for their high cost is that opihi must be chiseled off rocks, and it's a dangerous business: I know because I love to dive for them. Despite the local axiom, never turn your back on the ocean, amateur opihi harvesters regularly get swept out to sea and drown. I created this signature dish after trying an oyster shooter served in a tomato cocktail sauce at a local Mexican restaurant. I decided to use the delicately flavored tomato water that I always keep on hand to give it a distinctively Asian twist. I originally used small Pacific oysters for this recipe, but then I tried opihi, which works perfectly with the burst of heat from the wasabi. Try two $1/4$-inch cubes of ripe mango as a vegetarian alternative to the opihi.

1 tablespoon wasabi powder

$1/2$ teaspoon water

4 niçoise olives, pitted

16 Slivered Scallions (page 175)

8 paper-thin slices fennel bulb

4 chiso leaves, thinly sliced

4 fresh basil leaves, thinly sliced

4 Ume plums, minced

$1/2$ ripe tomato, diced into 16 pieces

4 opihi, or Belon, Kumamoto, or Olympia oysters, freshly shucked

$1/2$ cup Infused Tomato Water (page 176)

4 sprigs chervil

In a small bowl, mix the wasabi with the water. Form the paste into 4 pearl-sized balls.

To assemble the shooter, in fluted 2-ounce shooter or shot glasses, add in the following order: an olive, 2 scallion slivers, 2 fennel slices, a sliced chiso leaf, a sliced basil leaf, an Ume plum, 4 tomato dice, 2 scallion slivers, an opihi, a wasabi pearl, 2 tablespoons of tomato water, and a chervil sprig. Do not press the ingredients in the glass when assembling or they will not leave the glass easily. Consume the contents of the glass in one gulp.

YIELD: 4 SERVINGS

Oysters on the Half Shell
with Tomato–Chile Pepper Water Ice

The first time I ever ate an oyster was at culinary school. Back then I thought the oyster was a weird-looking creature. I felt it was looking back at me while I was looking at it, and I really didn't know if I wanted to eat it! Now I love oysters, especially the Belon variety from Europe and those from the Pacific Northwest and New Zealand. Today, oysters are even being raised on the Big Island. This dish marries this briny delicacy with something distinctively Hawaiian, shave ice. Instead of the traditional sweet, syrupy, and brightly colored ice, this is a subtly and deliciously flavored savory version.

SAVORY SHAVE ICE

2 cups Infused Tomato Water
  (page 176)

1/2 tablespoon Chile Pepper Water
  (page 175)

2 cloves garlic, thinly sliced

8 fresh basil leaves, rubbed

1/4 cup thinly sliced funnel bulb

Salt and pepper to taste

4 cups coarse rock salt

2 teaspoons black peppercorns
  (optional)

2 teaspoons green peppercorns
  (optional)

2 teaspoons red peppercorns
  (optional)

16 oysters, freshly shucked on
  the half shell

1/3 cup wasabi tobiko

In a bowl, combine the Infused Tomato Water, Chile Pepper Water, garlic, basil, fennel, and salt and pepper. Let sit for 1 hour for the flavors to develop. Strain. Discard the garlic, basil, and fennel. Freeze for 4 hours, but every 20 to 30 minutes or so as the liquid freezes, whisk to make the ice crystals flaky and fluffy and appear like finely shaved ice.

To serve, place 1 cup of rock salt on each plate, sprinkling the peppercorns over for colorful presentation. Arrange the oysters on the rock salt and top each oyster with 1 tablespoon of the shave ice and 1 teaspoon of the wasabi tobiko.

YIELD: 4 SERVINGS

Nori-Wrapped Tempura Bigeye Tuna with Tomato-Ginger Relish and Soy-Mustard Sauce

This dish is a perfect example of modern Hawaii Regional Cuisine: the combination of Hawaii's varied ethnic culinary influences (including Chinese, Japanese, and Filipino, as well as local), high-quality local ingredients, contemporary cooking methods, and, in my case, classical European (and especially French) training. Although this recipe involves several steps and the preparation of individual components, I promise that the different flavors come together in a very exciting fashion. The proof of any dish is in the eating, and this one tastes wonderful!

SOY-MUSTARD SAUCE

2 tablespoons hot water

4 tablespoons Coleman's dry mustard

4 tablespoons Yamasa soy sauce or other brand

1 cup white wine

$1/4$ cup white wine vinegar

3 tablespoons minced shallots

3 white peppercorns, crushed

$1/2$ cup heavy cream

$1/2$ pound cold butter, cut into 8 pieces

Salt and white pepper to taste

TEMPURA BATTER

2 eggs

$1 3/4$ cups ice-cold water

2 cups all-purpose flour

4 (3-ounce) ahi tuna fillets

2 nori sheets, halved

4 tablespoons wasabi paste

Vegetable oil for deep-frying

$1/4$ cup all-purpose flour

1 cup Tomato-Ginger Relish (page 131)

1 teaspoon black sesame seeds, for garnish

To prepare the sauce, in a bowl, whisk together the water and mustard to form a smooth paste. Slowly stir in the soy sauce until thoroughly combined. In a saucepan over medium-high heat, bring the wine, vinegar, shallots, and peppercorns to a boil. Cook until the liquid is reduced to about $1/4$ cup. Add the cream, return to a boil, and cook until again reduced to $1/4$ cup (the mixture will be thick enough to coat the back of a spoon). Remove from the heat and whisk in the butter, allowing each piece of butter to melt before adding more, until it is all incorporated. Season with salt and pepper and strain into a clean saucepan. Slowly add the soy-mustard mixture and stir until thoroughly incorporated. Keep warm; this sauce should not be refrigerated or reheated.

To prepare the batter, in a mixing bowl, beat the eggs. Whisk in the ice-cold water. Stir in the flour just until smooth. It is fine if the batter is a little lumpy; do not overwhisk or the mixture will become heavy.

Lay the nori on a work surface and spread the wasabi over the nori. Place the ahi across the short side of each piece of nori and roll up.

In a deep fryer or large saucepan over high heat, heat about 3 inches of vegetable oil to 350°. Sprinkle the flour on a plate. Lightly dip the nori roll in the flour and then the tempura batter. Deep-fry in the hot oil for about 45 seconds, or until the outside is crisp. Remove and drain on paper towels.

To serve, spoon $1/4$ cup of the relish in the center of each plate. Cut each roll into $1/4$-inch lengths. Arrange the slices around the relish. Carefully drizzle $1/2$ cup of the sauce around the slices. Garnish the sauce with the sesame seeds.

YIELD: 4 SERVINGS

Tempura—the technique for dipping foods in a batter and deep-frying—was actually introduced to Japan by Spanish and Portuguese traders in the sixteenth century. The Japanese refined and perfected the technique as we know it today.

AHI POKE PLATTER

Poke (pronounced "poh-keh") is derived from the Hawaiian word meaning "small cut pieces or cubes." Typically, the main ingredient of poke is cubed pieces of fresh raw fish such as tuna (yellowfin ahi is the most popular), aku (skipjack tuna), swordfish, or marlin. No question, the emphasis is on the word "fresh" when it comes to the main ingredient of poke.

Centuries ago, for the first poke, Hawaiians used nets and spears to catch reef fish such as manini and enenue, which were hacked or scored with sharp tools made with stone or shell, and then cured with salt. Sometimes, the cured fish was mixed with toasted ground *inamona* (kukui nut) and *limu kohu* (seaweed). Special fish such as awa raised in fish ponds for the *ali'i*, or royalty, were also made into poke. Limited mostly to coastal waters in their canoes, ancient Hawaiians did not catch and consume much deep-sea fish or use it for poke as we do today.

(continued opposite)

Ahi Poke Nigiri

Serve poke individually as a starter or simultaneously or sequentially for a special poke brunch, lunch, or dinner. This recipe and those that follow all feature fresh sashimi-grade ahi tuna. The portions were designed to be served together on individual plates.

Nigiri is the term used in Japanese cuisine for the style of hand-rolled torpedo- or football-shaped sushi made with rice and topped with a slice of seafood such as ahi tuna. In this Hawaiian version, I substituted poke for the rice and then topped it with fresh ahi. The poke recipe yields more than needed for this recipe, but you can use the rest for the following poke recipes. If storing, refrigerate and use by the next day at the latest. You can also top mixed greens with any leftover poke for a quick and delicious salad.

AHI POKE

12 ounces sashimi-grade ahi tuna, finely diced

$^1/_2$ cup Slivered Scallions (page 175)

$^1/_2$ cup minced white onion

2 tablespoons chopped ogo (seaweed)

$^1/_2$ teaspoon chile sauce with garlic (such as Sambal Oelek)

1 teaspoon dark sesame oil

$^1/_2$ teaspoon inamona (optional)

$^1/_2$ teaspoon rock salt

1 tablespoon vegetable oil

4 chiso leaves

1 ounce sashimi-grade ahi, cut into 4 rectangular slices (about 2 inches by 1 inch)

1 tablespoon Soy-Mustard Aioli (page 183)

1 teaspoon wasabi tobiko

To prepare the poke, in a bowl, combine the tuna, scallions, onion, ogo, chile sauce, sesame oil, inamona, and rock salt. Take 1 to 1 $^1/_2$ tablespoons of poke in your hand. Gently squeeze and form into a torpedo- or football-shaped piece. Make 4 pieces.

Heat the vegetable oil in a sauté pan over high heat and sear the poke until browned on the outside but still rare in the middle, 30 to 40 seconds.

Divide the poke pieces among individual plates. Top each with a chiso leaf and ahi slice. Drizzle with the aioli and garnish with the wasabi tobiko.

YIELD: 4 SERVINGS

Seared Ahi Poke Cakes on Crostini

I enjoy creating dishes with crostini—thin slices of toasted bread—as much as I do eating them. Crostini provide a crispy, crunchy foundation for appetizers, and when combined with a softly textured topping like this melt-in-the-mouth poke, they can yield a delicious and interesting contrast of textures.

$^1/_4$ cup Ahi Poke (page 54)

1 cup olive oil

4 (3-inch) slices French baguette, cut on the diagonal

4 chiso leaves

4 thin slices tomato

2 teaspoons Chile Pepper Aioli (page 183), for garnish

2 teaspoons tobiko, for garnish

8 chives, or 2 teaspoons thinly sliced scallions, for garnish

Form the poke into 4 patties about 1 inch in diameter (using a 1-inch ring mold will make them neatly uniform). Refrigerate until needed.

In a sauté pan over medium heat, heat the olive oil until hot. Sauté the bread slices for about $1^1/_2$ to 2 minutes on each side, or until golden. Drain on paper towels.

Divide the crostini among individual plates. Top each with a chiso leaf and tomato slice. In a clean nonstick sauté pan over medium-high heat, sear the poke patties for 10 seconds on each side. Place a patty on top of each tomato slice. Garnish with a dollop of the aioli, a dollop of the tobiko, and the chives.

YIELD: 4 SERVINGS

Inamona is a traditional Hawaiian seasoning made from the nut of the official state tree, the kukui or candlenut. The tree was brought to the islands from Polynesia by ancient Hawaiians. The nuts, which are high in oil, are toasted, pounded, and mixed with salt. They are used most often with poke or as a condiment for raw fish. Roasted sesame oil makes a good substitute.

Poke in its present form and as a commonly served appetizer is a relatively recent innovation. Nowadays there are countless varieties of poke made from fish, shellfish, and even vegetables. Seasonings typically include different types of seaweed, scallions, onion, soy sauce, and chile powder. Some poke is even cooked.

Ahi Poke Gyozas with
Soy-Vinegar Chile Dipping Sauce

Gyozas (pronounced "ghee-oh-zuhs") are the Japanese version of potstickers and they are one of my all-time favorites. In this recipe, they are sautéed and then steamed, which gives the outside a crispy textural contrast to the silky ahi poke filling. The flavorful dipping sauce has just enough spice to keep your taste buds tantalized.

SOY-VINEGAR CHILE DIPPING SAUCE

1/4 cup white wine vinegar

1 cup Yamasa soy sauce or
   other brand

3 tablespoons Chile Pepper Water
   (page 175)

2 tablespoons freshly squeezed
   lemon juice

1/2 cup water

1 tablespoon minced garlic

1 teaspoon shichimi togarashi,
   or 1/2 teaspoon cayenne

12 round wonton wrappers

3/4 cup Ahi Poke (page 54)

2 tablespoons olive oil

1 1/2 cups water

12 mizuna leaves, for garnish

1/2 teaspoon black sesame seeds,
   for garnish

4 teaspoons tobiko, for garnish

To prepare the dipping sauce, in a bowl, combine the vinegar, soy sauce, Chile Pepper Water, lemon juice, water, garlic, and shichimi togorashi or cayenne. Refrigerate until needed.

Lay the wonton wrappers on a flat work surface and place 1 tablespoon of the poke in the center of each wrapper. Lightly brush one edge of each wrapper with water. Fold the wrapper over the filling to form a half-moon, and press the edges to seal. In a sauté pan over medium heat, heat the olive oil. Add the gyozas, and when browned, add the water. Cover and steam about 2 to 3 minutes, or until the water has just evaporated. Remove the cover and continue to cook for 1 to 2 minutes, or just until the gyozas are crispy on the bottom.

Divide the gyozas among individual bowls with the crispy side facing up. Garnish with the mizuna, sesame seeds, and tobiko. Accompany with the dipping sauce.

YIELD: 4 SERVINGS

*Clockwise from left: Seared Ahi Poke Cakes
(page 55), Ahi Poke Gyozas (this page),
Ahi Poke Nigiri (page 54).*

Mediterranean Summer Rolls:
Seared Ahi with Tapenade and Pesto

This is another recipe typical of Hawaii Regional Cuisine that merges the Asian concept of summer rolls using seared ahi, a Hawaiian favorite, with the intensely flavored Mediterranean components of pesto and tapenade. I created this colorful dish for the "Cuisines of the Sun" event in 1993, which had a Mediterranean theme. My mission, as the resident culinary chameleon of this extraordinary culinary series, was to develop an East-West menu featuring the flavors and ingredients of the southern European coastal region. This was one of the popular results.

TOMATO–CHILE PEPPER VINAIGRETTE

1 (5-ounce) tomato at room temperature, cored, seeded, and chopped

$1/2$ tablespoon minced garlic

$1^{1}/2$ tablespoons Chile Pepper Water (page 175)

$1/4$ cup olive oil

Salt to taste

$1/4$ cup olive oil

12 ounces sashimi-grade tuna, cut into slices about 6 inches long, $3/4$ inch across, and $3/4$ inch thick

$1/4$ cup shichimi togarashi

4 (6-inch) sheets rice paper

10 tablespoons Black Olive Tapenade (page 135)

4 fresh basil leaves

4 chiso leaves

1 cup julienned cucumber

8 sprigs mizuna lettuce

4 slices avocado

12 thin tomato wedges

$1/4$ cup Basil–Macadamia Nut Pesto (page 134)

To prepare the Tomato–Chile Pepper Vinaigrette, in a blender, combine the tomato, garlic, and Chile Pepper Water and purée until smooth. With the machine running, slowly add the oil until incorporated. Season with salt. Refrigerate until needed.

In a sauté pan over medium-high heat, heat the olive oil. Season the tuna with the shichimi, add to the pan, and sear for 10 seconds on each side. Transfer to a plate and refrigerate to stop the cooking process.

In a shallow bowl of hot water, immerse a sheet of rice paper for 5 seconds. Drain on a damp towel. Lay the paper on a flat work surface. Spread 1 tablespoon of the tapenade in a 4-inch circle in the center of the sheet. Add 1 basil and 1 chiso leaf, $1/4$ cup of the cucumber, 2 sprigs of mizuna, 1 slice of avocado, and one-quarter of the tuna. Lift one side of the rice paper and begin rolling it up. Tuck in the ends and roll up tightly, being careful not to tear the rice paper. Slice the roll on an angle into 2 even halves. Repeat for the remaining rolls.

Divide the rolls among individual plates. Spread about $1/2$ tablespoon of the remaining tapenade onto each tomato wedge and arrange 3 wedges on each plate. Pour the vinaigrette around the rolls and place the pesto decoratively in small dollops around the plate.

YIELD: 4 SERVINGS

Tropical Sea Beachee Martini

The title of this recipe is a play on words: the Hawaiian beach raw bar meets the ceviche concept. The pan-Asian ingredients give the ceviche an interesting and refreshing twist. I created this appetizer-in-a-martini-glass for a stand-up reception, and it's amazing how much more convenient and stylish this ceviche is to eat compared to one served on a boring old plate! If you prefer, you can use raw ono, swordfish, or scallops instead of the lobster.

1 stalk lemongrass

¹/₂ cup chopped lobster tail meat

3 kaffir lime leaves, julienned

3 fresh basil leaves, julienned

1 ripe tomato, diced

3 tomatillos, husked, rinsed, and diced

2¹/₃ cups finely diced pineapple

1¹/₄ cups finely diced mango

¹/₂ cup diced red onion

2 tablespoons freshly squeezed orange juice

2 tablespoons freshly squeezed lime juice

2 tablespoons freshly squeezed lemon juice

2 tablespoons olive oil

2 tablespoons Chile Pepper Water (page 175)

1 tablespoon Thai fish sauce

2 tablespoons minced garlic

Salt to taste

Cut 3 pieces from the stalk of lemongrass, each about 1 inch long. Using the flat side of a large knife or heavy skillet, flatten the pieces.

Blanch the lobster meat in a saucepan of boiling salted water for 10 seconds. Remove with a wire mesh strainer and cool in an ice bath.

In a bowl, combine the lemongrass, lime leaves, basil, tomato, tomatillos, pineapple, mango, onion, orange juice, lime juice, lemon juice, olive oil, Chile Pepper Water, fish sauce, garlic, the blanched lobster, and salt. Marinate for 1 hour to "cook" the lobster in the fruit acids. Remove the lemongrass.

To serve, divide among large martini glasses.

YIELD: 4 SERVINGS

Nairagi and Kajiki Carpaccio with Swordfish Poke and Soy-Chile-Lime Dressing

Because of their meaty consistency, both nairagi and kajiki make a wonderful fish carpaccio, my take on the classic Italian preparation of thinly pounded, seasoned raw beef. The dressing, daikon sprouts, chiso, and sashimi-style tuna all give this recipe a distinctly Japanese twist. Swordfish, ono (wahoo), or ahi can be substituted for the marlin.

4 ounces nairagi (striped marlin), cut into pieces measuring 5 inches long, 3 inches across, and 2 inches thick

4 ounces kajiki (blue marlin), cut into pieces measuring 5 inches long, 3 inches across, and 2 inches thick

SOY-CHILE-LIME DRESSING

³/4 cup Yamasa soy sauce or other brand

¹/2 cup Chile Pepper Water (page 175)

¹/2 cup freshly squeezed lime juice

¹/2 cup water

CRISPY CHEESE WAFER

1 cup grated Parmesan cheese

1 teaspoon furikake

SWORDFISH POKE

6 ounces swordfish, finely diced

¹/4 cup Slivered Scallions (page 175)

¹/4 cup minced white onion

1 tablespoon chopped ogo (seaweed)

¹/4 teaspoon chile sauce with garlic (such as Sambal Oelek)

¹/2 teaspoon dark sesame oil

¹/4 teaspoon inamona (optional)

¹/4 teaspoon rock salt

Salt and pepper to taste

4 teaspoons olive oil

4 teaspoons capers, rinsed and drained

4 teaspoons daikon sprouts

4 teaspoons minced white onion

1 cup mixed greens, such as lolla rossa, frisée, and mizuna

Tightly wrap the nairagi and kajiki in plastic wrap and freeze for at least 30 minutes and preferably overnight.

To prepare the dressing, in a bowl, combine the soy sauce, Chile Pepper Water, lime juice, and water.

To prepare the wafer, sprinkle the cheese evenly in a 6-inch nonstick pan and place over medium-low heat for 2 minutes, or until it melts together in a sheet and begins to bubble. Sprinkle with the furikake. Turn out onto a flat plate and let cool. Once hardened, cut into 4 pieces.

To prepare the poke, in a bowl, combine the swordfish, scallions, onion, ogo, chile sauce, sesame oil, inamona, and rock salt. Refrigerate until needed.

Using an electric slicer, cut the nairagi and kajiki against the grain as thinly as possible. Alternatively, cut the fish into slices and lightly pound between sheets of plastic wrap until very thin. Season with salt and pepper.

Layer the nairagi and kajiki alternately on individual plates. Evenly spread the olive oil, capers, sprouts, and onion over the fish. Mound the swordfish poke in the center of the carpaccio and top with the greens. Sprinkle with the dressing and top with the cheese wafer.

YIELD: 4 SERVINGS

Nairagi, the Japanese name for striped marlin, and *kajiki,* or Pacific blue marlin, are lean, firm-fleshed types of billfish with tunalike consistency and a clean, almost sweet taste. The orange-hued nairagi is a little more robustly flavored than the white-fleshed kajiki.

Mushroom-Stuffed Lobster
with Lobster Vinaigrette

This elegant dish is simpler than it may seem at first glance. It may sound surprising that cold-water Maine lobster is being raised in Hawaii, but it's true, and it's a little sweeter than "wild" lobster.

LOBSTER VINAIGRETTE

1 tablespoon butter

1 tablespoon all-purpose flour

1 cup Lobster Stock (page 177)

Salt and white pepper to taste

$1/4$ cup tarragon vinegar

$1^1/2$ cups olive oil

2 lobsters, about $1^1/2$ pounds each

LOBSTER STUFFING

6 tablespoons Garlic Butter (page 181)

8 shiitake mushrooms, sliced

$1/2$ cup enoki mushrooms, cut into 2-inch lengths

$1/4$ cup chopped fresh flat-leaf parsley

20 asparagus spears, about 3 inches long

1 tablespoon vegetable oil

$1/4$ cup Thyme and Red Bell Pepper Butter (page 182)

4 tat soi leaves, or 4 sprigs watercress, for garnish

2 tablespoons Basil Oil (page 181)

To prepare the lobster vinaigrette, in a saucepan over low heat, melt the butter. Add the flour and stir to thoroughly incorporate. Whisk in the lobster stock a little at a time, increase the heat to medium-high, and bring the sauce to a boil. Then reduce the heat and simmer for 20 minutes. Season with salt and pepper, strain into a stainless steel bowl, and let cool over an ice bath. In a blender, combine the stock mixture and vinegar and purée until thoroughly combined. With the machine running, slowly add the oil until incorporated. Refrigerate until needed.

Bring a stockpot of salted water to a boil. Add the lobsters and boil for 1 minute. Remove from the pan and separate the head, arms, and claws from the tails by pulling them apart. Reserve the heads for stock or freeze them for later use. Return the arms and claws to the boiling water and cook for 7 minutes. Let cool to room temperature (do not refrigerate or the meat will toughen). Crack open the shells and reserve the meat. Split the lobster tails down the middle (with the shell still attached) and set aside at room temperature.

Preheat the oven to 350°.

To prepare the stuffing, in a sauté pan over medium heat, melt $1/4$ cup of the Garlic Butter. Add the mushrooms, the cooked meat from the lobster arms and claws, and parsley. Sauté for 2 to 3 minutes. Remove from the heat and keep warm.

In a sauté pan over medium heat, melt 2 tablespoons of the Garlic butter. Sauté the asparagus for 3 or 4 minutes. Remove from the heat and keep warm.

In an ovenproof skillet or sauté pan over high heat, heat the vegetable oil. Sprinkle the lobster tails with a pinch of salt and sear, meat side down, for 2 to 3 minutes. Spread 2 tablespoons of the Thyme and Red Bell Pepper butter on each tail and return to the pan, meat side up. Roast for 5 minutes.

Remove the lobster tails from the oven and partially remove the meat from the shell by curling the tail end up and away from the shell. Spoon the warm lobster stuffing into the shells. To serve, place the lobster tails on individual plates. Arrange the asparagus around the lobster and garnish with the tat soi, placing it between the shell and the meat. Pour 1 tablespoon of the vinaigrette and $1/2$ tablespoon of the Basil Oil around each plate.

YIELD: 4 SERVINGS

Salmon "Pork Rinds" Wrapped in Chiso with Salmon Tartar

In the South, as well as the Philippines, crispy roast pork skin is considered by many to be a delicacy. Here, the fattier part of the salmon, the belly, which is little used in restaurants, makes an excellent appetizer. The fresh salmon tartar, salmon caviar, and the aromatic chiso leaf provide a contrasting balance of texture and flavor. If chiso is unavailable, wrap the salmon inside a butter lettuce leaf and use a combination of fresh basil and mint in each package. *(Recipe pictured on page iii.)*

6 ounces scaled salmon belly (about 5 inches long and ³/₄ inch thick)

Salt to taste

¹/₂ teaspoon vegetable oil

SALMON TARTAR

8 chiso leaves

4 ounces minced fresh salmon

¹/₂ cup minced sweet Maui onion

2 tablespoons minced capers

2 tablespoons freshly squeezed lemon juice

¹/₂ teaspoon salt

1 teaspoon wasabi powder

¹/₂ teaspoon water

1 tablespoon sour cream

2 tablespoons salmon caviar (ikura)

Cut the salmon belly into 6 pieces approximately ³/₄ inch square and season both sides with salt. In a sauté pan or skillet over low heat, heat the oil. Sauté the salmon for about 15 minutes, or until crispy like bacon.

To prepare the salmon tartar, mince 2 of the chiso leaves. In a bowl, combine the minced chiso, salmon, onion, capers, lemon juice, and salt.

In a separate bowl, mix the wasabi and water to form a thick paste.

To assemble the "rinds," place one of the chiso leaves on each plate. Put a piece of crispy salmon at the stem end of each leaf. Top with 1 teaspoon of the tartar and ¹/₂ teaspoon of the sour cream. Fold the end of the chiso leaf over the salmon and sour cream. Accompany with the salmon caviar and a small dollop of wasabi paste.

YIELD: 6 SERVINGS

The Ocean Thermal Energy Conservation (OTEC) facility, on the Big Island's Kona coast, pipes cold ocean water from a depth of 2,000 feet to generate electricity. A by-product of this process is nutrient-rich cold water, which is distributed to local oyster, shrimp, salmon, and seaweed farmers, and my good friend Joe Wilson. Joe, whom we affectionately call "the lobster man," raises top-quality Maine lobsters and is able to supply us year-round. Joe raises his Maine lobsters in water with a constant temperature of 33–35°; it takes his lobsters about three years to reach maturity, which is less than half the time it takes in the wild.

"Poky Pines": Crispy Ahi Poke with Avocado, Wasabi Soy Sauce, Togarashi Aioli, and Tarragon-Tobiko Vinaigrette

The spiky centerpiece of this dish—poke deep-fried inside a wild-looking package of won-ton strips—looks like a pair of hyper porcupines, hence the name. This recipe is a good example of how I create some of my dishes: I like to play with ingredients in the kitchen, and sometimes I feel like a child experimenting with his toys. If I like the way the flavors combine, and the whole dish makes sense, I look for a way to make an attractive presentation. In this case, I was experimenting with wrapping poke and noticed some deep-fried wonton strips we had on hand. These ingredients inspired this recipe, and I liked the strikingly unusual result. Fortunately, our guests at Alan Wong's feel the same way, and the poky pines are now a signature item on the menu.

WASABI SOY SAUCE

2 tablespoons wasabi powder

3 tablespoons hot water

3 tablespoons Yamasa soy sauce or other brand

TOGARASHI AIOLI

$^1/_2$ cup Aioli (page 182)

$^1/_2$ tablespoon shichimi togarashi

1 tablespoon red wine vinegar

8 square wonton wrappers

Cornstarch for sprinkling

1 cup Ahi Poke (page 54)

Vegetable oil for deep-frying

1 avocado, peeled, pitted, and halved

$^1/_4$ cup Tarragon Vinaigrette (page 32)

4 amaranth leaves or watercress sprigs, for garnish

To prepare the wasabi soy sauce, in a bowl, combine the wasabi, water, and soy sauce. Refrigerate until needed.

To prepare the aioli, in a bowl, combine the plain aioli, shichimi togarashi, and vinegar. Refrigerate until needed.

On a flat work surface, stack the wrappers, sprinkling a little cornstarch between each one so they do not stick. Cut into long, thin strips and divide into 8 even piles. Using your hands, shape the poke into 8 compact, golf ball–sized balls. Press 1 side of the strips around the outside of 1 poke ball with the ends sticking upright. Repeat for the remaining poke strips.

In a deep fryer or large saucepan over high heat, heat about 3 inches of vegetable oil to 350°. Using tongs or chopsticks, gently lower the poky pines, one at a time, into the hot oil. Keeping them upright, deep-fry about 45 seconds, or until golden brown. Remove and drain on paper towels.

Quarter each avocado half, thinly slice to form a fan, and arrange on individual plates. Place 2 dollops of the aioli in the center of each plate and put a poky pine on top of each dollop. Drizzle the vinaigrette and wasabi soy sauce around each plate. Place an amaranth leaf or watercress sprig between the poky pines.

YIELD: 4 SERVINGS

Salads from the Garden

Salads from the Garden

Salads are wonderfully versatile dishes—an important part of a healthy diet. Salads can be enjoyed as a starter, a light lunch, an accompaniment to dinner, or as a palate cleanser between courses. I enjoy creating them because they offer a wealth of opportunities to contrast textures, flavors, colors, and even temperatures. Salads can also be used to showcase particular ingredients, whether seasonal favorites or extraordinary elements, such as fresh hearts of palm, our excellent Hawaiian seafood, or vine-ripened tomatoes bursting with flavor. Most importantly to me, salads provide an opportunity to create beautiful presentations that please the eye as much as the palate.

Lettuce greens are an important part of the showcase. I am proud to say that most of the salad greens that we use at Alan Wong's are grown by Kurt and Pam Hirabara on their farms in Hilo and Waimea on the Big Island, not far from the active Kilauea volcano. For the Hirabaras, growing their "babies," as they call them, is a labor of love. The care and pride they take in their work is unmistakable, and it rubs off on the work that we do with their produce. Many of our salads use a Mediterranean-style mesclun mix of young greens—*mesclun* is a word in the southern French dialect meaning "mixture." Mesclun greens are widely available year-round. They are flavorful, bite-sized, and tender, with no wasteful tough or stemmy parts.

When preparing salads, remember that quality is paramount. Unless you use appealing, ripe produce, the results will fall short. It's usually best to skip a salad rather than settle for second-best produce. This may mean that you should wait to enjoy your favorite salad until the ingredients are in season.

"Ahi Cake": Eggplant Layered with Ahi Tuna, Maui Onions, and Tomatoes with Puna Goat Cheese Dressing

This light and refreshing terrine-like salad is assembled in a bowl so that it looks like a cake when unmolded; hence its name. When cut, the colorful layers are revealed, which together with the complex combination of flavors and textures, makes it a great recipe for entertaining.

The dressing recipe yields substantially more than you will need for this dish, but it just doesn't taste the same if it's made in any smaller quantity. It also works perfectly with the Puna Goat Cheese and Tomato Salad (page 79) and keeps indefinitely in the refrigerator.

CHILE-LEMONGRASS DRESSING

$1/4$ cup freshly squeezed lime juice

$1/2$ cup Yamasa soy sauce or other brand

$1/2$ cup water

$1/2$ cup sugar

1 tablespoon Thai fish sauce

1 minced Hawaiian chile or red serrano chile

$1/4$ cup minced lemongrass

2 tablespoons plus 1 teaspoon minced ginger

1 tablespoon minced garlic

4 ounces Puna goat cheese

1 (12-ounce) eggplant, cut into $1/8$-inch-thick slices

6 tablespoons olive oil

2 sweet Maui onions, cut into $1/8$-inch-thick slices

Salt to taste

8 ounces sashimi-grade ahi tuna, cut into $1/4$-inch-thick slices

3 vine-ripened tomatoes, cut into $1/8$-inch-thick slices

$1/2$ cup firmly packed fresh basil leaves

$1/4$ cup Tomato-Ginger Coulis (page 44)

8 sprigs basil, for garnish

To prepare the dressing, in a bowl, combine the lime juice, soy sauce, water, sugar, fish sauce, chile, lemongrass, ginger, and garlic. Place the goat cheese in a mixing bowl and slowly whisk in $1/4$ cup of the dressing to form a paste. Whisk until any lumps are eliminated. Refrigerate until needed. Reserve the remaining Chile-Lemongrass dressing for another use.

Prepare the grill. Place the eggplant and onion slices on paper towels. Lightly sprinkle with salt and let sit for 10 minutes.

Brush the eggplant with 2 tablespoons of the olive oil and sprinkle with salt. Grill the eggplant for 2 to 3 minutes on each side, or until tender (alternatively, it can be sautéed or broiled). Remove the eggplant and refrigerate until needed. In a saucepan over medium-high heat, heat 2 tablespoons of the olive oil. Add the onion to the pan and sauté for 4 to 5 minutes, or until tender. Refrigerate until needed.

Lightly season the ahi with salt. In a sauté pan over high heat, heat 2 tablespoons of the olive oil. Sear the ahi for 5 seconds on each side. Refrigerate immediately to stop the cooking process.

Line a 3-cup bowl with plastic wrap. Cut out a circle of cardboard the size of the top of the bowl and wrap with plastic wrap. Working in a circular pattern, layer the salad in the following order: half the tomatoes, one third of the eggplant, one third of the onions, half the basil, 1 tablespoon of the olive oil, half the ahi, half the remaining eggplant, half the remaining onion, the remaining basil, the remaining ahi, the remaining eggplant, the remaining onion, and the remaining tomatoes. Place the cardboard inside the bowl and cover with a weight. Refrigerate for 30 minutes. Drain the juices from the bowl, unmold the cake, and slice into 8 portions.

Pour 2 tablespoons of the dressing into each individual shallow bowl and spread in a circle. Arrange a slice of the ahi cake in the center of each bowl and carefully dot or drizzle $1/2$ tablespoon of the coulis around the edge of the dressing. Garnish with a basil sprig.

YIELD: 8 SERVINGS

Mixed Greens, Oranges, Fennel, and Herbs with Asiago and Lemon–Macadamia Nut Oil Vinaigrette

The light, refreshing flavors of the greens and the orange segments in this Mediterranean-style salad emphasize the theme of tasty, healthful foods from sunny climates. For a shortcut, substitute 6^1/$_2$ cups of mesclun mix for the mixed greens. *(Recipes containing uncooked eggs are not recommended for immuno-compromised individuals or small children.)*

LEMON–MACADAMIA NUT OIL VINAIGRETTE

1 egg

^{1}/$_4$ cup freshly squeezed lemon juice

2 teaspoons minced garlic

2 tablespoons minced shallot

2 cups macadamia nut oil

2 teaspoons salt

Up to ^{1}/$_4$ cup water

2^1/$_2$ cups gently packed lolla rossa or red oak lettuce

^{2}/$_3$ cup gently packed tat soi or baby spinach

^{2}/$_3$ cup gently packed mizuna lettuce

^{2}/$_3$ cup gently packed baby arugula

1 cup gently packed radicchio

1 cup gently packed frisée, yellow ends only

^{1}/$_2$ cup very thinly sliced fennel bulb

^{1}/$_4$ cup gently packed fresh basil leaves

^{1}/$_4$ cup gently packed chervil sprigs

2 oranges, peeled, pith removed, and separated into 20 sections

^{1}/$_2$ cup shaved Asiago cheese

To prepare the vinaigrette, in a blender, combine the egg, lemon juice, garlic, and shallots and purée for 45 seconds to 1 minute. With the machine running, slowly add the oil until incorporated. Season with the salt. If the mixture becomes too thick, add water until the mixture is thin enough to be poured. Refrigerate until needed, and up to 2 weeks.

In a bowl, combine the salad greens, fennel, and herbs. Toss with the vinaigrette.

To serve, arrange 5 orange segments around the perimeter of each plate. Divide the greens among the plates. Top with the cheese.

YIELD: 4 SERVINGS

Chinese Roasted Duck Salad with Endive, Green Beans, and Hoisin-Balsamic Vinaigrette

Roasted duck and the sweet, sour, and piquant hoisin sauce are flavorful partners, as the classic Chinese dish of Peking Duck proves. Since Peking Duck is one of my favorite foods, I wanted to create a salad that echoed those wonderful flavor combinations. The hoisin in the vinaigrette is further enhanced by the balsamic vinegar, rice wine vinegar, garlic, and mustard, making a tantalizing combination on the palate. The European ingredients in this salad—endive and haricots verts—successfully balance the Asian components, with the bitter endive cutting the richness of the duck and the crunch of the beans providing a textural counterpoint. Another key to this recipe is the temperature contrast achieved by serving the duck warm.

HOISIN-BALSAMIC VINAIGRETTE

2 tablespoons Dijon mustard

2 tablespoons aged balsamic vinegar

1 tablespoon rice wine vinegar

6 tablespoons hoisin sauce

1/2 teaspoon minced garlic

1/2 teaspoon minced ginger

2 teaspoons minced shallots

1/2 cup peanut oil

1/4 cup olive oil

Salt to taste

20 haricots verts, trimmed

20 snow peas, trimmed

4 cups mixed greens

20 endive leaves

1 cup bean sprouts

8 ounces sliced roast duck, warmed

2 teaspoons sliced scallions, green parts only

8 sprigs cilantro

1/2 teaspoon white sesame seeds, toasted

To prepare the vinaigrette, in a blender combine the mustard, vinegars, hoisin sauce, garlic, ginger, and shallots and purée until smooth. With the machine running, slowly add the oils until incorporated. Season with salt. Refrigerate until needed.

In boiling salted water, blanch the haricots verts for about 2 minutes and the snow peas for 1 minute. Transfer to an ice bath to cool.

In a bowl, combine the haricots verts, snow peas, greens, endive, sprouts, and duck. Toss with 1/2 cup of the vinaigrette.

To serve, divide the salad among individual plates. Top with the scallions, cilantro, and sesame seeds.

YIELD: 4 SERVINGS

Mixed Greens with
Warm and Cold "Seafood Salad"

The words *seafood salad* often conjure up images of heavy mayonnaise-bound salads made with macaroni or potato—as often as not with pieces of imitation crab. Well, this light, refreshing recipe is far from that stereotype, with not a drop of mayo or a strand of pasta to be found! This is a salad of many interesting contrasts, between the cold and warm seafood; between the soft shrimp and lobster and chewy tako and calamari; and between the creamy avocado and papaya and the crunchy beans and the crisp greens. If you cannot find tako, substitute poached snapper or salmon or more calamari.

1 cup water

Juice of 1/2 lemon

1 teaspoon peppercorns

1 bay leaf

2 ounces calamari

2 teaspoons olive oil

4 jumbo shrimp, peeled and deveined

1/2 teaspoon salt

4 cooked lobster claws, meat removed
    and shells discarded

2 tablespoons Garlic Butter (page 181)

12 asparagus spears, trimmed to
    4 inches (optional)

12 haricots verts

1 1/2 ounces sashimi-grade ahi tuna,
    diced

2 ounces cooked tako (octopus),
    thinly sliced

1/2 cup diced avocado

4 cups mixed lettuce greens

1/2 cup diced papaya

1/2 cup Tarragon Vinaigrette
    (page 32)

4 sprigs chervil, for garnish

1 tablespoon chives, sliced into
    1-inch lengths, for garnish

In a saucepan, bring the water, lemon juice, peppercorns, and bay leaf to a boil. Add the calamari and remove from the heat. Let sit for 5 minutes. Drain the calamari and slice into 1/4-inch-thick rings.

In a sauté pan over medium-high heat, heat the olive oil. Sprinkle both sides of the shrimp with the salt and sear for 1 minute, or until they turn pink and are almost cooked. Add the lobster meat and Garlic Butter and sauté for about 2 minutes, or until the butter melts and the shrimp are cooked through. Remove from the heat.

In a saucepan of boiling salted water, blanch the asparagus for 3 minutes and the haricots verts for 2 minutes. Transfer to an ice bath to cool.

In a bowl, combine the shrimp, lobster, asparagus, tuna, tako, avocado, mixed greens, and papaya. Add the vinaigrette and toss well.

To serve, divide the salad among individual plates, making sure each plate has 1 shrimp and 1 lobster claw; arrange the lobster so it is sticking up vertically from the salad. Garnish with the chervil and chives.

YIELD: 4 SERVINGS

Calamari is the Italian name for squid. It's called *ika* in Japan and is a much-used seafood in most Asian cuisines. Squid is at its most tender when 2 inches long or less. When cooked, it has a firm texture with a chewy quality, and a pleasant, mild flavor. In Hawaii, squid is sometimes made as a luau dish, cooked with coconut milk, coconut, and taro leaves.

Vertical Tomato Salad:
Sliced Vine-Ripened Tomatoes and Maui Onions with Tapenade and Macadamia Nut Pesto

This salad always gets a reaction because of its unusual and striking presentation. Each tomato is sliced horizontally and then arranged with onion and basil fins. Viewed from above, the tomato looks as if it's about to fly off the plate! The vinaigrette, tapenade, and pesto complement the straightforward flavors of the tomato salad perfectly. I prefer the tomatoes tennis-ball size, but if they are smaller, the recipe will still work just fine. This recipe just doesn't work without top-quality, vine-ripened tomatoes.

4 (5-ounce) vine-ripened tomatoes

1 small sweet Maui onion

16 fresh basil leaves

1 cup Tarragon Vinaigrette (page 32)

2 teaspoons aged balsamic vinegar

4 teaspoons Basil Oil (page 181)

4 teaspoons Basil–Macadamia Nut Pesto (page 134)

4 teaspoons Black Olive Tapenade (page 135)

We are fortunate at the restaurant that Richard and Patsy Nakano supply us with the best tomatoes I've tasted. Their Nakano Farms is located on the dry side of Kamuela on the Big Island, and their red, yellow, gold, and green tomatoes grow in greenhouses under carefully controlled conditions. They also raise wonderful Japanese cucumbers, French beans, and watercress. Richard is a retired county extension agent from the University of Hawaii and knows more about local agriculture on the Big Island than anyone else I know.

Score the bottom of each tomato with an X. In a saucepan of boiling water, blanch each tomato for 10 seconds. Transfer to an ice bath. When cool, carefully peel the tomatoes, keeping the flesh perfectly smooth. Cut each tomato into 5 horizontal slices. Keep the slices of each tomato stacked together.

Halve the onion lengthwise and then halve again. Thinly slice these quarters into 16 half-moons about the same size. Mince some of the remaining onion to yield 4 teaspoons and reserve.

To assemble each salad, place the bottom slice of a tomato on each plate. Add an onion half-moon so that it is half sticking out beyond the edge of the tomato slice and a basil leaf next to it arranged at 45° to the onion. Add another slice of tomato, directly over the first slice. Add another onion half-moon at 45° to the basil leaf below it (that is, at 90° to the onion below), sticking out the same way. Add another basil leaf at 45° to the onion half-moon you have just added. Add another tomato slice, onion half-moon, and basil leaf in the same way. Cover with the top slice of the tomato. Viewed from the top, the tomato will look like a pinwheel, with the onion and basil sticking out at regular intervals.

Pour $1/4$ cup of the vinaigrette around each salad. Accent the vinaigrette with drops of the balsamic vinegar and basil oil. Place 1 teaspoon each of the pesto, tapenade, and minced onion on each plate.

YIELD: 4 SERVINGS

"Stacked" Eggplant and Puna Goat Cheese Salad

This brightly flavored Mediterranean-style salad features eggplant and tomatoes, both members of the nightshade family. Most people think of eggplant as a vegetable, but like the tomato, it is a fruit. Salting the eggplant and letting it sweat for 10 minutes causes it to release some of its juices, resulting in a more tender texture when cooked.

CROUTONS

4 slices French bread, angle-cut $1/8$ inch thick and 5 to 6 inches long

$1/4$ cup olive oil

1 (12-ounce) Italian eggplant, cut into 8 slices

$1/2$ teaspoon salt

$1/4$ cup olive oil

2 vine-ripened tomatoes, each cut into 4 slices

$1/4$ cup Basil–Macadamia Nut Pesto (page 134)

1 cup Puna goat cheese or other good-quality mild chevre

$1/2$ cup Mediterranean Relish (page 132)

$1/2$ Ka'u orange or regular orange, peeled, pith removed, and separated into 8 segments

8 sprigs chervil

4 teaspoons balsamic vinegar

4 teaspoons Basil Oil (page 181)

To prepare the croutons, lay the bread slices horizontally on a flat work surface and cut each slice at a diagonal so the 8 pieces are pointed at one end and curved at the other. In a sauté pan over medium-high heat, heat the olive oil until hot. Fry the bread about 20 seconds on each side, or until they turn golden brown and the pointed ends turn inward.

Place the eggplant slices on paper towels. Lightly sprinkle with salt and let sit for 10 minutes. Place the eggplant in a mixing bowl and pour the olive oil over the eggplant. Prepare the grill (alternatively, the eggplant may be sautéed) and soak some wood chips. Grill the eggplant over the wood chips at medium-high heat until the slices are fully cooked and feel dry, about 2 minutes on each side.

To assemble the salad, place a $2^1/2$-inch-diameter cylinder mold or cookie cutter on each plate. Fill in the following order: 1 slice tomato, 1 slice eggplant, 1 tablespoon pesto, $1/4$ cup goat cheese, 1 slice tomato, 1 slice eggplant, and 2 tablespoons of the rel-ish. Press down lightly to compress the stack. Place 1 crouton upright in the center of the stack.

Arrange 2 orange segments on each plate, one on each side of the crouton, and 1 sprig of chervil on each orange segment. Carefully remove the mold. Drizzle each plate with 1 teaspoon of the balsamic vinegar. Accent the vinegar with 1 teaspoon of the Basil Oil.

YIELD: 4 SERVINGS

Eggplant is native to India and Southeast Asia, where it has been cultivated for thousands of years. Arabian traders brought it to Europe in medieval times. Later, Thomas Jefferson introduced it to the United States. The elongated Japanese eggplant was probably the first type brought to Hawaii by immigrants in the nineteenth century.

Puna Goat Cheese and Tomato Salad with Chile-Lemongrass Dressing

This recipe is labor intensive, but don't be intimidated, because it's straightforward and well worth the effort. The salad features the contrasts of textures, flavors, and colors that I love to create in my recipes. The secret is in cutting the tomato as finely as possible. It is an elegant salad that cannot be made ahead of time.

4 ounces Puna goat cheese or other good-quality mild chèvre

1 1/2 tablespoons minced garlic

Salt and white pepper to taste

16 haricots verts

4 (5-ounce) tomatoes

1/2 small sweet Maui onion, sliced

2 teaspoons black sesame seeds

1/2 cup Chile-Lemongrass Dressing (page 70)

1 Ka'u orange or regular orange, peeled, pith removed, and separated into sections

20 mizuna lettuce or arugula leaves, for garnish

In a bowl, season the goat cheese and garlic with salt and pepper. Refrigerate until needed.

In a saucepan of boiling water, blanch the haricots verts for 2 minutes. Drain and halve.

Core the tomatoes. Using a very sharp knife, slice the tomatoes lengthwise as thinly as possible. To assemble the salads, carefully and gently fan the tomato slices so they overlap and form a circle on each plate. Place the haricots verts and onion in the center of each circle. Using 2 large spoons, shape the cheese mixture into 4 oval shapes. Roll the top of each cheese ball in 1/2 teaspoon of the sesame seeds so they adhere in a strip. Carefully place the cheese on top of the haricots verts and onion. Drizzle with Chile-Lemongrass Dressing. Arrange the orange sections on either side of the cheese. Garnish with the mizuna or arugula.

YIELD: 4 SERVINGS

Shrimp and Big Island Hearts of Palm Salad

Hearts of palm are harvested from the peach palm, a multistemmed plant that is not destroyed when the hearts are cut. Fresh hearts of palm are becoming increasingly available in many markets (Costa Rica and Brazil are the main exporters of hearts of palm), whereas twenty years ago, they could only be purchased in canned form. Trial plantations have been established in the Islands by the University of Hawaii's College of Agriculture with a view to growing fresh hearts of palm on a commercial basis. Because one of the goals of Hawaii Regional Cuisine is diversifying top-quality local produce, this is a very promising development.

10 to 12 ounces fresh hearts of palm, about 20 (2-inch-long) pieces

4 cups water

Juice of 1 lemon

2 bay leaves

$1/2$ cup white wine

$1/2$ tablespoon peppercorns

1 tablespoon salt

8 jumbo shrimp, heads attached

2 cups firmly packed lolla rossa or red oak lettuce

$1/4$ cup firmly packed mizuna lettuce or mustard lettuce

$1/4$ cup firmly packed arugula or watercress

$1/4$ firmly packed tat soi or baby spinach

$1/4$ cup firmly packed frisée

$1/4$ cup Tarragon Vinaigrette (page 32)

$1/4$ cup Balsamic Rum Syrup (page 39) (optional)

$1/4$ cup Basil Oil (page 181) (optional)

$1/4$ cup Tomato–Chile Pepper Vinaigrette (page 58)

16 sprigs chervil, for garnish

In a steamer basket set in a saucepan of boiling water, steam the hearts of palm for 10 minutes. When cool, remove the tough outer layer of skin. Trim so that one end is even and the other is angled. Refrigerate until chilled.

In a saucepan, bring the water, lemon juice, bay leaves, wine, peppercorns, and salt to a boil. Add the shrimp and simmer for about 4 minutes, or until the shrimp is pink and cooked through. Peel and devein the shrimp. Refrigerate until chilled.

In a bowl, combine the lolla rossa, mizuna, arugula, tat soi, and frisée. Toss lightly with the Tarragon Vinaigrette.

To serve, divide the greens among individual plates. Arrange 5 pieces of hearts of palm, standing upright, around each salad and top with 2 shrimp. Drizzle the Balsamic Syrup, Basil Oil, and Tomato–Chile Pepper Vinaigrette around the plate. Garnish with the chervil.

YIELD: 4 SERVINGS

The Hukilau:
Main Courses from the Sea

The Hukilau:
Main Courses from the Sea

The hukilau is an enduring social and cultural tradition linking Hawaiians with the ocean that has sustained them over the centuries. Like the luau, camaraderie and a sense of community plays a big part in the hukilau. In the past, the hukilau was a harvesting occasion that involved an entire fishing community (*huki* means "pull" and *lau* means "ropes" in Hawaiian). Large seine nets (in Hawaiian, *'upena paloa*) made from native fibers and vines were used. The nets, averaging 200 feet in length with a half-inch mesh, held taut with wooden floats and stone sinkers, were put out from the shore or set from canoes. Several hours later, everyone helped to pull in the net and land the catch. The fish were then divided between all who had taken part, and often a big feast was held. This celebration of group spirit is considered just as important as the catch and the feast itself.

Seafood has always been an important source of protein in the Hawaiian diet. On average, Hawaiians still consume twice as much seafood as people in the rest of the United States. This reflects availability and quality as well as habit and personal preferences. Hawaii has some of the best fish in the world swimming in the offshore waters, and the Honolulu fish market is the second largest in the country.

As a chef, the bountiful variety of fresh seafood represents an exciting challenge to match the range of flavors and textures with other ingredients while letting the inherent qualities of the seafood shine. It takes practice and skill to learn how to best cook different fish, and that is another part of the challenge I enjoy. For example, while some delicate fish are best steamed, you would never consider cooking ahi tuna this way, and instead you would grill or pan-sear it, rather like beef steak. Judging the window of opportunity for doneness—what the French refer to as *à point* ("to the point")—is also an acquired art that makes cooking seafood so much fun. It's a case of timing, looking at the fish, touching it, and drawing on your experience to know when the moment has come to put it on the plate.

Following these recipes will add to your experience and enhance your knowledge of cooking fish, and I hope you will find I am passing on a little of that "acquired art." I also hope you will approach these recipes this way—as opportunities to learn and perfect the craft of cooking the freshest fish you can find. Then, in the spirit of the Hawaiian hukilau, share and enjoy the results with your family and friends.

Steamed Opakapaka and
Gingered Vegetables in Truffle Broth

Opakapaka, or pink snapper, is a popular Hawaiian deepwater fish that is sometimes served raw for sashimi. Its meat is leaner in summer and a little more fatty in the winter months. When steamed as in this recipe, opakapaka's light, flaky, moist texture and natural flavor shine through. When cooking fish, it's tempting to overgild the lily, but it's important to know when to leave well alone. The combination of soy and truffles works wonderfully well and ties the other ingredients and flavors together.

SHRIMP AND PORK HASH

1 pound shrimp, shelled, deveined, and ground

1 pound pork

1 egg

$^1/_2$ cup fresh water chestnuts, finely diced, or canned

1 tablespoon minced garlic

$^1/_2$ cup finely sliced scallions, green parts only

$^1/_4$ cup oyster sauce

1 teaspoon dark sesame oil

Salt and pepper to taste

OPAKAPAKA

$^1/_4$ cup tapioca pearls

1 pound opakapaka fillet, boneless and skinless, cut into 8 portions about 3 inches long, 1 inch wide, and 1 inch thick

3 cups hot Chicken Stock (page 177)

$^1/_2$ cup truffle butter

Salt to taste

1 cup sliced Chinese mustard cabbage (kai choy) or bok choy

1 cup sliced won bok or napa cabbage

$^1/_4$ cup julienned red onion

$^1/_4$ cup bean sprouts

$^1/_2$ cup peanut oil

1 teaspoon finely julienned ginger

1 teaspoon finely julienned scallion, white parts only

2 tablespoons Yamasa soy sauce or other brand

2 tablespoons Slivered Scallions (page 175), for garnish

8 sprigs cilantro, for garnish

24 paper-thin slices truffle, for garnish (optional)

To prepare the hash, in a bowl, combine the shrimp, pork, egg, water chestnuts, garlic, scallions, oyster sauce, sesame oil, salt, and pepper. Refrigerate until needed.

In a small saucepan over medium heat, bring 2 cups of water to a boil. Add the tapioca pearls and boil for 12 to 15 minutes, or until clear and translucent, stirring occasionally to prevent the tapioca from sticking. Strain the tapioca and reserve.

Divide the shrimp hash into 8 portions and place each between 2 pieces of opakapaka laid on a work surface in a V shape. For each portion, compress the fish together to completely enclose the hash. Wrap a strip of foil around each shrimp and hash portion, folding so it is only as high as the fish. Secure the foil by crimping the ends to form a "package."

Transfer the opakapaka "packages" to a lightly buttered saucepan large enough to fit them in a single layer. Carefully add 2 cups of the chicken stock and 2 tablespoons of the truffle butter, and over medium-high heat, bring the stock to a boil. Lower the heat to medium and simmer the fish for 5 to 7 minutes, or until perfectly tender. Divide the fish among warm individual serving plates. Stir the remaining 2 tablespoons of the truffle butter into the saucepan and season the sauce with salt.

Meanwhile, in a small saucepan over medium heat, heat the remaining 1 cup of chicken stock, add the tapioca pearls, and warm through. Place the mustard cabbage, won bok, onion, and bean sprouts in a steamer or vegetable basket and set in a saucepan of lightly boiling water. Cover and steam for 3 minutes, or until tender. Meanwhile, in a small saucepan over medium-high heat, heat the peanut oil until almost smoking. Transfer the steamed vegetables to a bowl, top with the ginger and scallion, and drizzle with the soy sauce. Pour the hot oil over the top.

Place the vegetables on top of the fish and garnish with the scallions and cilantro. Spoon the sauce around the fish and arrange the tapioca pearls next to each serving. Garnish the sauce with the truffle slices.

YIELD: 4 SERVINGS

Tempura Ono on Sweet-and-Sour Lilikoi Sauce with Thai Cucumber Salsa

Ono, called wahoo in other parts of the United States, is the most elegant member of the mackerel family and also one of the largest. Because the ono has a low fat content, it is best not to grill or sauté it as direct heat will dry it out. Instead, it is best crusted or cooked in a batter, which seals the moisture and delicate flavor inside, or poached. Without doubt, ono is my favorite type of fish to cook in a batter. This recipe will also work with other firm-fleshed white fish such as mahi mahi, halibut, or sea bass. It follows the Chinese tradition of serving whole fish with a sweet-and-sour sauce. I love using the wonderful local *lilikoi*, or passion fruit, in my recipes. The fish and the sweet-and-sour flavors in this recipe are counterbalanced by the spicy salsa.

SWEET-AND-SOUR LILIKOI SAUCE

1/2 cup frozen passion fruit concentrate

1/2 cup plus 1 tablespoon water

1/2 cup sugar

1/2 cup white vinegar

1/2 teaspoon dark sesame oil

1 tablespoon cornstarch

3 cups all-purpose flour

2 cups water

2 eggs

Vegetable oil for deep-frying

24 ounces ono fillet, cut crosswise into 12 pieces

24 bamboo skewers (8 to 10 inches in length)

Thai Cucumber Salsa (page 130)

1 teaspoon black sesame seeds, for garnish

8 sprigs cilantro, for garnish

4 sprigs basil, for garnish

To prepare the sauce, in a small saucepan over medium heat, bring the passion fruit concentrate, 1/2 cup of the water, the sugar, vinegar, and sesame oil to a boil. In a cup, mix the cornstarch and the remaining 1 tablespoon of water. Add to the pan and stir for 1 minute. Keep warm.

In a bowl, combine 2 cups of the flour, the water, and eggs. Whisk to form a batter. Refrigerate until needed.

In a deep fryer or large saucepan, heat about 3 inches of vegetable oil to 350°. Divide the ono among the skewers. Dredge in the remaining cup of flour and dip into the batter. Deep-fry the ono for about 3 minutes, or until the batter is golden brown and the ono is cooked through.

To serve, divide the salsa among individual plates. Pour the sauce around the salsa. Garnish the sauce with the sesame seeds, cilantro, and basil. Arrange 3 of the ono skewers in a tepeelike design on each plate.

YIELD: 4 SERVINGS

Ginger-Crusted Onaga with Corn, Mushrooms, and Miso-Sesame Vinaigrette

This signature item is the single most popular dish on the menu at Alan Wong's. Perhaps that is because onaga happens to be my favorite fish. I promise that it is the most succulent, tender, and sweet fish you'll ever have the pleasure of eating. Almost any white, firm-fleshed fish will work in this recipe, especially halibut, but onaga really is the best. The ginger crust is so *ono*—or delicious—I eat it on its own with rice. The crust was inspired by my childhood memories of Chinese cold ginger chicken. The vinaigrette makes a perfect marriage with the onaga, and although it has a creamy consistency, it contains no dairy. *(Recipes containing uncooked eggs are not recommended for immuno-compromised individuals or small children.)*

MISO-SESAME VINAIGRETTE

1/2 cup rice wine vinegar

1/4 cup Chicken Stock (page 177)

3 tablespoons white miso

3 tablespoons sugar

2 egg yolks

2 tablespoons chunky peanut butter

2 teaspoons minced ginger

1 teaspoon minced garlic

1 Hawaiian red chile or serrano chile, minced

2 teaspoons Dijon mustard

1 cup vegetable oil

2 tablespoons dark sesame oil

2 teaspoons white sesame seeds, toasted

Up to 1/2 cup water

1/4 cup peanut oil

4 (7-ounce) onaga fillets

Salt and pepper to taste

1/2 cup Ginger-Scallion Oil (page 180)

1/2 cup panko

2 teaspoons butter

1/4 cup sliced shiitake mushrooms

1/4 sliced enoki mushrooms

1/2 cup corn kernels (from 1 ear corn)

1/4 cup Basil Oil (page 181)

4 teaspoons Slivered Scallions (page 175)

2 teaspoons black sesame seeds

Preheat the oven to 350°.

To prepare the vinaigrette, in a bowl, combine 1/4 cup of the rice wine vinegar, the stock, miso, and sugar. In a blender, combine the remaining 1/4 cup of rice wine vinegar, the egg yolks, peanut butter, ginger, garlic, chile, and mustard and purée until smooth. With the machine running, slowly add the vegetable oil until incorporated, and then slowly add the sesame oil. Stir in the sesame seeds. If the mixture seems too thick, add water until the mixture can be poured. Add the blended mixture to the bowl and stir thoroughly. Refrigerate until needed.

In a sauté pan over high heat, heat the peanut oil until hot. Season the onaga with salt and pepper. When the oil is almost smoking, sear the onaga for about 45 seconds on each side, or until brown. When cool, top the onaga with the Ginger-Scallion Oil (including the solids it contains) and dust on one side with the panko. Transfer the onaga to an ovenproof skillet or roasting pan. Bake for 6 minutes, or until tender and cooked through.

Meanwhile, in a sauté pan over medium heat, melt the butter. Add the mushrooms and sauté for 3 to 4 minutes, or until they soften and begin to brown. Add the corn and sauté for 2 minutes longer, or until the corn is slightly tender.

To serve, divide the sautéed vegetables among individual plates. Pour 1/2 cup of the vinaigrette around the vegetables and drizzle the Basil Oil over the vinaigrette. Place the onaga on the vegetables and top with the scallions. Sprinkle the sesame seeds around the plate.

YIELD: 4 SERVINGS

Onaga is the Japanese name for the long-tailed red snapper. Hawaiians call it *'ula'ula*. It is caught in deep water and is especially plentiful in the winter months.

Seared Peppered Yellowfin Ahi and Crispy Asian Slaw

Pairing tuna and soy is common here in Hawaii—and not just on sushi plates. Any good-quality tuna can be used for this recipe. The inspiration for the crispy slaw and soy vinaigrette was my memory of Chinese chicken salads and Japanese somen salads. The cilantro, scallion, and ginger give the slaw a fragrance that is an integral part of the dish and complements its many flavors and textures.

SOY VINAIGRETTE

$^1/_4$ cup water

$^1/_2$ cup Yamasa soy sauce or
    other brand

$^1/_4$ cup vegetable oil

$^1/_4$ cup rice wine vinegar

$^1/_4$ cup mirin

$^1/_4$ cup sugar

2 cloves garlic, halved

2 tablespoons minced ginger

$^1/_4$ teaspoon sesame oil

2 tablespoons freshly squeezed
    lime juice

1 red Hawaiian chile or
    serrano chile, minced

CRISPY ASIAN SLAW

Vegetable oil for deep-frying

4 wonton wrappers

2 teaspoons cornstarch

$^1/_4$ cup julienned ginger

2 cups julienned Chinese or
    napa cabbage

$^1/_2$ cup julienned purple cabbage

$^1/_2$ cup julienned snow peas

$^1/_2$ cup carrots, julienned

1 tablespoon minced cilantro

12 asparagus spears, trimmed to
    3 inches

4 (8-ounce) yellowfin ahi tuna steaks

Salt and crushed peppercorns to taste

3 tablespoons peanut oil

4 teaspoons Slivered Scallions
    (page 175)

To prepare the vinaigrette, in a bowl, combine the water, soy sauce, oil, vinegar, mirin, sugar, garlic, ginger, sesame oil, lime juice, and chile. Refrigerate for at least 30 minutes to allow the flavors to marry. Strain and stir before using.

To prepare the slaw, in a deep fryer or large saucepan over high heat, heat 3 inches of vegetable oil to 350°. Sprinkle the wonton wrappers with the cornstarch to keep them from sticking. Stack and julienne the wonton wrappers. Deep-fry the wonton wrappers for about 15 seconds, until golden and crisp. Remove and drain on paper towels. Add the ginger to the oil and deep-fry until golden and crispy, about 1 minute; take care as the ginger burns easily. Remove and drain on paper towels.

In a bowl, combine the cabbages, the snow peas, carrots, cilantro, vinaigrette, and wonton wrappers and toss together carefully.

In a saucepan of boiling salted water, blanch the asparagus for 2 minutes. Drain and transfer to an ice bath to cool.

Cut each ahi steak into quarters about 1 inch thick and season with the salt and peppercorns. In a sauté pan over high heat, heat the peanut oil. Sear the ahi for about 45 seconds on each side for medium-rare.

Arrange 3 asparagus spears on each plate with the tips pointing out from the center. Place the ahi in the center of the plate, covering the stem end of the asparagus. Mound 2 cups of the slaw on the ahi. Top with the deep-fried ginger and the scallions.

YIELD: 4 SERVINGS

Yellowfin tuna is the type of tuna most favored for sashimi and many kinds of seared or lightly cooked dishes because of its flavor. The aku or skipjack tuna is often preferred for poke, and the fattier, whiter albacore is most commonly used for canned tuna. Tuna tends to be more abundant in the summer months in Hawaiian waters, although ocean temperatures, currents, and feeding conditions all affect migration patterns. Much of the commercial catch is made in deep waters from longline boats, sometimes several hundred miles from Hawaii. Occasionally, yellowfin of over 200 pounds are landed, but usually they average 100 pounds.

Grilled Mahi Mahi and
Stir-Fried Vegetables with Wasabi Sauce

Mahi mahi is a great eating fish, with a firm, moist texture and slightly sweet flavor. This is one of the few recipes in which we use butter—it forms a perfect marriage in the sauce with the pungent wasabi and salty soy sauce.

WASABI SAUCE

2 tablespoons wasabi powder

4 tablespoons hot water

2 tablespoons Yamasa soy sauce or other brand

1 cup Beurre Blanc (page 182)

2 tablespoons peanut oil

20 snow peas

3 cups chopped won bok

1 cup chopped choy sum

2 cups chopped Chinese mustard cabbage (kai choy)

1 cup bean sprouts

1 red onion, sliced

¹/₄ cup Yamasa soy sauce or other brand

1 teaspoon dark sesame oil

4 (7-ounce) mahi mahi fillets

Salt to taste

Vegetable oil for the grill

1 tablespoon wasabi powder

¹/₄ cup warm water

4 teaspoons Slivered Scallions (page 175), for garnish

1 teaspoon black sesame seeds, for garnish

Prepare the grill.

To prepare the wasabi sauce, in a bowl, whisk together the water and wasabi to form a smooth paste. Slowly stir in the soy sauce until thoroughly combined. Slowly add the wasabi mixture to the Beurre Blanc and stir until thoroughly incorporated. Keep warm.

In a wok or large sauté pan over high heat, heat the oil. Add the snow peas, won bok, choy sum, mustard cabbage, bean sprouts, and onion. Stir together and add the soy sauce. Caramelize for about 45 seconds. Add the sesame oil and remove the wok from the heat.

Season the mahi mahi with salt. Brush the grill with vegetable oil to prevent the fish from sticking. Grill the mahi mahi for 4 to 5 minutes on each side, or until cooked through.

In a small bowl, combine the wasabi powder and water to form a paste.

To serve, divide the vegetables among individual plates. Place the mahi mahi on the vegetables. Pour ¹/₂ cup of the Wasabi Sauce around the vegetables. Place 5 dollops of the wasabi paste on the sauce on each plate. Garnish with the scallions. Sprinkle the sesame seeds around the plate.

YIELD: 4 SERVINGS

Mahi mahi, also known as dolphin-fish and dorado, is a striking-looking creature in the water—its silvery skin has an iridescent blue-green tint and its belly is bright yellow-gold. Some say it's one of the most beautiful of all ocean fish. It's found in tropical waters around the world and is abundant in Hawaiian waters.

Steamed Moi with Shrimp Hash, Roots Salad, and Ponzu Sauce

The moi is a delicately flavored type of sea bream that held a special importance in ancient Hawaii. Moi is hard to catch in the wild and subject to strict seasons. For this recipe, you can substitute trout. The crunchy vegetable salad was inspired by a delicious Japanese raw potato salad I enjoy.

PONZU SAUCE

$^1/_2$ cup Yamasa soy sauce or other brand

$^1/_2$ cup water

$^1/_3$ cup yuzu

$^1/_4$ cup freshly squeezed orange juice

$^1/_4$ cup freshly squeezed lime juice

ROOTS SALAD

1 cup finely julienned peeled raw potato

1 cup finely julienned peeled raw beet

1 cup finely julienned peeled raw carrot

1 cup finely julienned peeled raw celeriac

$^1/_2$ cup Slivered Scallions (page 175)

4 (6-ounce) moi fillets

Salt and pepper to taste

Shrimp Hash (page 139)

4 chiso leaves (with buds attached, if available), or 4 teaspoons Slivered Scallions (page 175), for garnish

12 thin lime slices, for garnish

4 thin slices lotus root, for garnish

To prepare the ponzu sauce, in a bowl, combine the soy sauce, water, yuzu, orange juice, and lime juice.

To prepare the salad, rinse each julienned vegetable under running water to remove the starch and bleed the beet. Place in separate bowls of ice water to keep cold and crisp.

Season the moi fillets with salt and pepper. Line a well-oiled, 3-inch-deep, 4-inch-wide ring mold or large cookie cutter with the moi, skin side out. It is fine if the moi stands up above the rim of the mold. Spoon the Shrimp Hash into the mold, inside the moi. Place the mold in a steamer basket. In a saucepan of lightly boiling water, cover and steam the mold for 8 to 10 minutes, or until the fish and hash are fully cooked.

Carefully unmold the stuffed moi and transfer to individual plates. Arrange the potato, beet, carrot, celeriac, and scallions in layers on the moi. Spoon about $^1/_4$ cup of the sauce around each plate and about 1 tablespoon of the sauce on the vegetables. Garnish with a chiso leaf, lotus root slice, and 3 lime slices.

YIELD: 4 SERVINGS

Moi, or Pacific threadfin, was the most favored fish of the Hawaiian *ali'i*, or royalty, and a *kapu*, or royal taboo, prohibited commoners from eating moi at the risk of execution. Manmade saltwater fish ponds were built so that moi could be raised to satisfy the royal demand—a few of these fish ponds have been restored and are still used for aquaculture. According to Donald D. Kilolani Mitchell, in *Resource Units in Hawaiian Culture*, "The early Hawaiians built a greater number and a larger variety of fish ponds than did any other Pacific islanders. Their cultivation of food animals and plants in ponds was true aquaculture. About the year 1800 there were some 300 royal fish ponds producing food for the chiefs and kahuna."

Spiny Lobster with Lobster Wonton Ravioli in Curry Potato Sauce

Warm water spiny lobsters differ from cold water Maine lobsters in not having any claws, but their flavors are similar. This is an East-West dish: wonton ravioli that works very well with the rich, delicate lobster. The Thai-influenced sauce came about when I was experimenting with puréed chowders. The potato starch makes a natural thickener and creates a rich taste much like cream. This is also true of the Rice Cream on page 96. You can make this dish with any type of shellfish—shrimp, scallops, crayfish, clams, or mussels—or a firm-fleshed fish.

LOBSTER WONTON RAVIOLI

$^1/_2$ cup Lobster Mousse (page 31)

2 teaspoons minced fresh flat-leaf parsley

$^1/_2$ cup diced cooked lobster meat

16 square wonton wrappers or thin ravioli wrappers

2 eggs, whisked

2 (1$^1/_2$-pound) spiny lobsters

CURRY POTATO SAUCE

$^1/_4$ cup loosely packed cilantro

4 kaffir lime leaves

$^1/_2$ cup firmly packed fresh basil

$^1/_4$ cup sliced lemongrass

$^1/_2$ tablespoon minced garlic

$^1/_2$ tablespoon sliced jalapeño

1 tablespoon minced ginger

2 tablespoons peanut oil

$^1/_2$ tablespoon curry powder

2$^1/_2$ cups Chicken Stock (page 177)

$^1/_2$ cup canned unsweetened coconut milk

2 tablespoons Thai fish sauce

$^1/_4$ cup diced potato

1 tablespoon water

Salt to taste

2 tablespoons olive oil

$^1/_4$ cup fresh corn kernels (from $^1/_2$ ear corn)

16 snow peas, trimmed

$^1/_2$ cup quartered shiitake mushroom caps

8 sprigs basil

$^1/_4$ cup thinly sliced lemongrass

2 red Hawaiian chiles, thinly sliced, or 1 red serrano or Thai chile, minced

12 sprigs cilantro

4 kaffir lime leaves

To prepare the wonton ravioli, in a bowl, combine the Lobster Mousse, parsley, and lobster meat. Lay out the wonton wrappers on a flat work surface. Place 1 tablespoon of the lobster mixture in the center of each wrapper. Lightly brush the edges of the wrappers with the whisked egg and fold the wrapper over diagonally to form a triangle enclosing the filling. Press the edges of the wrapper to seal. Bring in the 2 far corners, add a little egg, and press together to seal. Bring a saucepan of water to a boil. Add the wontons and simmer for about 3 minutes. Drain and set aside.

To prepare the lobsters, bring a stockpot of salted water to a boil. Add the lobsters and boil for 15 to 17 minutes. Remove from the pan, cut in half lengthwise, and remove the coral and tomalley.

To prepare the sauce, in a food processor or blender, combine the cilantro, lime leaves, basil, lemongrass, garlic, jalapeño, and ginger and coarsely chop. In a saucepan over high heat, heat the peanut oil. When almost smoking, add the chopped cilantro mixture and fry about 2 minutes. Add the curry powder and cook for 30 seconds longer. Add the stock, coconut milk, and fish sauce and bring to a boil. In the food processor, purée the potato and water. Add to the saucepan and stir for about 3 to 4 minutes, or until the sauce thickens. Season with salt, strain, and set aside.

In a large saucepan over medium-high heat, heat the olive oil. Add the corn, snow peas, and mushrooms, and sauté for 2 to 3 minutes. Add the Curry Potato Sauce, simmer for 1 minute, and add the wonton raviolis. Cook until heated through.

Divide the sauce and wonton ravioli among large individual bowls. Place a lobster half on top of the sauce. Top with the basil, lemongrass, chiles, cilantro, and lime leaves.

YIELD: 4 SERVINGS

Furikake Salmon with
Ume Chiso Rice Cream on Linguine

Rice Cream is my contribution to smooth, healthy, low-fat, nondairy sauces. Its origin is rooted in my childhood: Whenever I felt sick, my mother would cook up some rice porridge, and it always did the trick. Many years later, I came to work feeling unwell and made some rice porridge for myself in the kitchen. I happened to be standing next to a blender and so I began experimenting by adding in some green tea, ume, and chiso leaf—familiar combinations in Japanese cuisine—included a little butter for extra richness, and this particular sauce was born. That night, I served Grilled Salmon with Get-Well Sauce! As time went by, I added more Rice Cream–based sauces to my repertoire. The rice makes a great medium for other flavors, and the consistency is similar to a rich butter or cream sauce but with less fat.

RICE CREAM

2 1/2 cups clam juice

2 1/2 cups Chicken Stock (page 177)

1/2 cup short-grain sticky white rice, rinsed

UME CHISO SAUCE

3 tablespoons ume paste, or
   2/3 ounce ume plums

1 chiso leaf

2 anchovies

1/4 teaspoon plus 1 tablespoon freshly squeezed lemon juice

1/2 cup softened butter

1/4 teaspoon salt

2 cups Tomato Water (page 176)

1 tablespoon olive oil

12 ounces fresh linguine

3 tablespoons vegetable oil

4 (6- to 8-ounce) boneless, skinless salmon fillets

5 teaspoons furikake

1/2 cup Lomi Tomato Relish
   (page 21)

4 teaspoons Slivered Scallions
   (page 175), for garnish

To prepare the Rice Cream, in a saucepan over high heat, bring the clam juice, stock, and rice to a boil. Reduce the heat and simmer, uncovered, for 20 to 30 minutes, or until the rice is tender, stirring occasionally so the rice does not stick. Transfer to a blender and purée. Strain 2 cups of the Rice Cream into a clean saucepan. The unused Rice Cream can be refrigerated and used (within 3 days) as a substitute for cream sauce in other recipes.

To prepare the sauce, in a food processor, combine the ume, chiso, anchovies, and 1/4 teaspoon of the lemon juice and process until finely chopped. Transfer to a bowl and add the butter. Stir together and season with salt. Add one half of the mixture to the saucepan with the Rice Cream. Add the Tomato Water and the remaining 1 tablespoon lemon juice to the saucepan. Stir well and heat until the butter is melted and the ingredients are thoroughly incorporated.

To prepare the linguine, in a saucepan of boiling salted water cook the olive oil and linguine for 1 to 2 minutes, or until al dente. Drain and keep warm.

In a large sauté pan over high heat, heat the vegetable oil. Season each salmon fillet with 1 teaspoon of the furikake. Sauté the salmon for 3 to 4 minutes on each side (depending on thickness), or until medium-rare. Dust the top side of each salmon fillet with the remaining teaspoon of the furikake.

To serve, divide the linguine among four serving plates and pour 1/2 cup of the sauce around each serving. Place the salmon on top of the linguine and top each fillet with 2 tablespoons of the relish. Garnish with the Slivered Scallions.

YIELD: 4 SERVINGS

For an optional attractive garnish, cut a strip of salmon skin into 4 pieces, each about 2 1/2 inches by 1 inch, trimming off any excess flesh. Place the skin on an oiled baking sheet and season with 1/4 teaspoon of salt. Preheat the oven to 350° and bake the salmon skin for about 10 minutes, or until golden brown and crispy. Cut into tall thin triangles and lean a triangle upright against each salmon fillet.

Sautéed Shrimp and Penne Pasta with Garlic Rice Cream

This simple yet delicious Mediterranean-style pasta dish includes a hint or two of Hawaii and shows the versatility of my Rice Cream as well as its ability to carry other flavors. The possibilities of Rice Cream combinations are endless. Just think of all the compound butter recipes that have ever been created, and then substitute the Rice Cream for the butter. You can use another type of pasta, but it should be substantial enough to hold the sauce and ingredients. If you prefer a dairy-free sauce, omit the Garlic Butter.

8 ounces dried penne pasta

$^1/_2$ cup olive oil

2 pounds jumbo shrimp (about 24), peeled and deveined

Salt and pepper to taste

1 cup all-purpose flour

4 teaspoons minced garlic

1 cup Chardonnay or other dry white wine

$1^1/_4$ cups Tomato Water (page 176)

2 tablespoons capers, rinsed

$^1/_4$ cup diced tomato

$^1/_4$ cup Garlic Butter (page 181)

$^1/_4$ cup chopped fresh flat-leaf parsley

$1^3/_4$ cups Rice Cream (page 96)

4 sprigs basil

4 teaspoons grated Parmesan cheese

$^1/_4$ cup Lomi Tomato Relish (page 21)

In a saucepan of boiling water, cook the pasta for 10 to 12 minutes, or until al dente. Drain and keep warm.

Meanwhile, in a large sauté pan over high heat, heat the olive oil. Season the shrimp with salt and pepper and lightly dredge in the flour. Sauté the shrimp for about 45 seconds on each side, or until golden brown. Add the garlic, wine, and Tomato Water and deglaze the pan. Add the capers, tomato, Garlic Butter, parsley, and Rice Cream. Continue to cook, stirring, until heated through. Add the cooked pasta and stir until it is well coated and warmed through.

To serve, divide the pasta among individual bowls. Top with the basil, cheese, and relish.

YIELD: 4 SERVINGS

Steamed Bowl of Shellfish: Lobster, Shrimp, and Clams in Hawaiian-Style Bouillabaisse with Chile Aioli and Roasted Garlic Smashed Potatoes

I'll let my sous chefs—the heart and soul of the kitchen at Alan Wong's—tell you about this bouillabaisse because they all have strong opinions about it. "This is my favorite dish to eat on the whole menu, bar none," says Barbara Stange, who has worked with me since I was at the Mauna Lani. "Of all the dishes I enjoy cooking, it's this one," Lance Kosaka tells me. "It really involves cooking skill, and using your judgment." Steven Ariel points out that it's not only a popular dish with our guests but a great value for seafood lovers. "The main thing is to organize all the ingredients," advises Steven. "Then it's relatively easy to finish. It must not be overcooked, so timing is all-important."

HAWAIIAN-STYLE BOUILLABAISSE

1 1/2 tablespoons olive oil

1/2 cup chopped celery

1/2 cup chopped onion

1/2 cup chopped leeks

1/2 cup chopped fennel bulb

1/4 cup chopped red bell pepper

1/4 cup dry white wine

1/4 teaspoon saffron

1/4 cup tomato paste

1 1/2 cups clam juice

4 cups Chicken Stock (page 177)

2 ounces mahi mahi or another firm-fleshed white fish, sliced

Salt and pepper to taste

1/4 teaspoon curry powder

1/8 teaspoon cayenne

1 teaspoon pernod

1 teaspoon brandy

2 lobster tails, cut in half lengthwise

8 ounces jumbo shrimp, peeled and deveined

20 fresh Manila clams, washed

12 sea scallops

2 Dungeness crabs, top shell and gills removed, cut into 4 pieces

Roasted Garlic Smashed Potatoes (page 137)

20 tat soi leaves

1/4 cup Chile Pepper Aioli (page 183)

1 teaspoon sliced chives

To prepare the bouillabaisse, in a large saucepan over medium heat, heat 1 tablespoon of the olive oil. Add the celery, onion, leeks, fennel, and bell pepper and sauté for 4 to 5 minutes, or until soft. Add the wine, saffron, tomato paste, clam juice, and stock. Bring to a boil and add the fish. Cook for about 5 minutes, or until the fish is cooked through. Season with salt and pepper.

Transfer the broth to a blender and purée. Return to a clean saucepan and bring to a simmer over medium heat. In a sauté pan over medium heat, combine the remaining 1/2 tablespoon olive oil, curry powder, and cayenne. Sauté for about 1 minute. Carefully add the pernod and brandy and stand well back as you ignite the liquor (the pan will catch fire). When the flames die down and the alcohol has burned off, stir the mixture into the broth in the saucepan.

Season the lobster tails with salt. With a medium strainer, strain about 4 cups of the broth into a clean large saucepan. Place over medium heat and add the lobster, shrimp, clams, scallops, and crabs. Simmer for 3 to 4 minutes, or until the shellfish is cooked. Discard any clams that do not open.

To serve, using a pastry bag, pipe 1 cup of the potatoes into the center of individual soup bowls. Divide the shellfish and broth among the bowls, standing the crab upright. Top the potato with the tat soi, placed upright. Drizzle 1 tablespoon of the aioli over the shellfish in each bowl. Sprinkle the chives over the bowls.

YIELD: 4 SERVINGS

Connoisseurs insist that the Marseilles region is the home of the authentic bouillabaisse, the saffron-flavored seafood stew from the southern coast of France. However, it's hard to imagine finer ingredients than those available in Hawaiian waters.

Thai Curry Crab-Crusted Shutome on Crispy Potato Pillows

Most of the shutome (Hawaiian swordfish) caught in local waters is exported to Japan, which is our loss. It's an underrated fish with a compact, meaty texture that stands up well to other flavors, as this recipe demonstrates. The crust transforms the shutome with the exotic flavors of Thailand, contrasting deliciously with the aromatic European-style vinaigrette and sauce. The crust, vinaigrette, and sauce can all be prepared up to 4 hours ahead. *(Recipes containing uncooked eggs are not recommended for immuno-compromised individuals or small children.)*

CRAB CRUST

1/4 cup canned unsweetened coconut milk

1/4 cup Chicken Stock (page 177)

3 kaffir lime leaves, minced

1 (4-inch) piece lemongrass, minced

1/2 teaspoon minced garlic

1/4 tablespoon minced ginger

1/2 teaspoon red Thai curry paste

1 teaspoon cornstarch

1 teaspoon water

1/4 cup butter, diced, at room temperature

5 fresh Thai basil leaves or regular fresh basil

2 teaspoons freshly squeezed lemon juice

2 teaspoons finely chopped red bell pepper

4 ounces crabmeat

2 tablespoons minced cilantro

FENNEL VINAIGRETTE

2/3 cup vegetable oil

2 tablespoons chopped fennel bulb

2 tablespoons white wine vinegar

1 egg yolk

2 pinches sugar

FENNEL-CUCUMBER SAUCE

2 tablespoons olive oil

2 tablespoons chopped fennel bulb

2 tablespoons chopped Japanese cucumber or English cucumber

1/2 tablespoon chopped cilantro

1/2 tablespoon freshly squeezed lime juice

1/8 teaspoon hot chile sauce

CRISPY POTATO PILLOWS

1 1/2 pounds potatoes, finely julienned

Vegetable oil for deep-frying

2 tablespoons vegetable oil

4 (7-ounce) shutome fillets

1 tablespoon Slivered Scallions (page 175), for garnish

To prepare the crust, in a small, heavy saucepan, bring the coconut milk and stock to a boil. Add the lime leaves, lemongrass, garlic, ginger, and curry paste. In a cup, mix the cornstarch and water and add to the pan. Bring the mixture to a boil, stirring constantly. Reduce the heat to very low. Add the butter and whisk until melted. Add the basil, lemon juice, and bell pepper and transfer to a bowl. When cool, add the crab and cilantro and combine thoroughly. Cover and refrigerate until needed.

To prepare the vinaigrette, in a blender, combine the oil, fennel, vinegar, egg yolk, and sugar. Purée until smooth. Transfer to a bowl. Refrigerate until needed.

To prepare the Fennel-Cucumber Sauce, in the blender, combine the oil, fennel, cucumber, cilantro, lime juice, and chile sauce and purée until smooth.

Preheat the oven to 450°.

To prepare the potato pillows, rinse the potatoes under cold running water to remove excess starch. In a deep fryer or large saucepan over high heat, heat about 3 inches of vegetable oil to 375°. Drain the potatoes and deep-fry for about 5 minutes, or until golden brown. Remove and drain on paper towels.

In a large, heavy skillet over high heat, heat the 2 tablespoons of vegetable oil. Add the shutome and sear for about 1 minute on each side. Transfer to a roasting pan and top with the Crab Crust. Bake for 10 minutes, or until the shutome is cooked through.

Bring the vinaigrette and purée to room temperature before serving. To serve, divide the vinaigrette among individual plates. Top with the shutome. Spoon dots of the purée on top of the vinaigrette around the fish and garnish the shutome with the scallions. Accompany with the potatoes.

YIELD: 4 SERVINGS

Steamed Ehu with Matsutake Mushroom Broth and Matsutake Flan

One of my favorite comfort foods is Chawan Mushi, a Japanese light savory egg custard that can be flavored in many different ways. This recipe is a takeoff of that dish. To serve this special-occasion dish, use attractive bowls measuring about 10 inches across and 3 inches deep. At the restaurant, we steam the bowls in a *bain marie*; if you don't own one, steam the bowls in large sauté pans or saucepans with water added carefully to come halfway up the sides of the bowls. Be sure the bowls are each covered with plastic wrap and the pans covered with foil.

MATSUTAKE BROTH

2 cups Chicken Stock (page 177)

2 cups sliced matsutake mushrooms
   (4 or 5 mushrooms)

1/4 teaspoon salt

MATSUTAKE FLAN

1 cup Chicken Stock (page 177)

2 eggs, beaten

1 tablespoon heavy cream

2 tablespoons sliced scallions,
   green parts only

1/4 teaspoon salt

1 pound ehu (short-tailed red
   snapper), skin on

2 (2- to 3-ounce) baby bok choy,
   halved

12 snow peas

4 shiitake mushroom caps

24 stems enoki mushrooms
   (about 1/4 ounce), for garnish

4 sprigs chervil or flat-leaf parsley,
   for garnish

To prepare the broth, in a saucepan over high heat, bring the stock to a boil. Add the mushrooms, reduce the heat to medium-low, and simmer for 20 minutes. Season with the salt. Strain through a fine mesh sieve and reserve the mushrooms and broth separately.

To prepare the flan, in a bowl, mix the stock, eggs, and cream. Add the scallions, cooked mushrooms, and salt. Set aside.

Cut the ehu at an angle into 1/4-inch-thick slices. Place the fish slices, skin side up, in a circular overlapping pattern in the center of individual bowls. Top each with a half bok choy, 3 snow peas, and shiitake mushroom cap. Carefully pour the flan mixture around the fish. Place a piece of plastic wrap securely over each bowl. Steam, covered, for 12 minutes (see recipe introduction), or until the fish is fully cooked and the flan is set.

Meanwhile, heat the reserved broth.

When the fish is cooked, carefully unwrap. Carefully ladle the hot broth over the flan and around the fish. Garnish with the enoki mushrooms and chervil or parsley.

YIELD: 4 SERVINGS

This is a fall and early winter dish for special occasions because of the seasonality and cost of *matsutakes*— Japanese wild mushrooms (literally pine mushrooms). The matsutakes, which can cost $60 per pound, have a slightly piney fragrance, meaty texture, and exquisite nutty flavor. Usually, they are available fresh at Japanese or gourmet markets. The quality of canned matsutakes is inferior, so I recommend substituting truffles or shiitakes.

From Mauka to Makai:
Main Courses from the Land

From Mauka to Makai: Main Courses from the Land

The title of this chapter, "From Mauka to Makai," meaning mountains to the sea, refers to both the land-based foods—that is, meat and vegetables—used in the recipes and to ancient boundaries in Hawaii. The district of each tribal chief included all the terrain, stretching from the mountain peaks to the shore, as well as all the animals it contained. Among the types of meat enjoyed by ancient Hawaiians were native birds such as *koloa* (duck), *nene* (goose), *moa* (chicken), and other forest birds; *pua'a* (pigs); and *ili'o* (dog). Chicken, pigs, and dogs had all been brought from Polynesia by the original settlers of the islands, and ownership was a sign of affluence. For the most part, meat was consumed by the nobility and higher social ranks, while the population at large ate mostly seafood. Meat of all kinds was usually cooked over hot coals in the *imu*, or underground oven.

After centuries of isolation, Hawaii was changed forever by Captain Cook's arrival in 1778. The influx of Europeans and Americans changed eating habits and practices radically. Many new animals and produce were introduced to the islands. In 1793, several breeding pairs of cattle and sheep were presented to King Kamehameha I by British naval Captain George Vancouver. These animals prospered in Hawaii's hospitable conditions, and livestock ranching soon became an important industry. From the mid-1850s into the twentieth century, successive waves of immigrants (mostly from Asia) brought new ingredients and cooking styles with them. During and after World War II, canned Spam (a pressed meat product) became popular in Hawaii. More Spam is consumed here, per person, than anywhere else, and it remains a firm local favorite, especially served with rice. Despite my promise to provide a complete range of Hawaii Regional Cuisine, I confess to offering no recipes for Spam here.

As for my formative years, my mother rarely cooked meat, and when she did, she might choose chicken or pork, but her preference was fish. Also common in Hawaii is teriyaki beef, hamburger steak, or beef stew, all with "two scoop rice and macaroni salad" for plate lunch.

You can imagine the speed of my learning curve once I decided to become a professional chef. At Lutèce, in New York City, one of my jobs was to butcher whole carcasses or large animal parts. This was invaluable experience; these days, butchering is becoming a lost art because of improved technology with vacuum wrapping and the convenience of using ready-to-cook portion-controlled cuts of meat. Butchering is one aspect of basic cooking knowledge, and a cooking skill that I teach the staff at Alan Wong's.

Drunken Duck on Choy Sum with Mushrooms and Roasted Garlic Smashed Potatoes

Travel is a great teacher, and this dish was inspired by a trip I took to Malaysia in 1991. At an outdoor cafe in Kuala Lumpur, I enjoyed a meal of whole duck cooked in medicinal herbs. Until then, I'd never tried—or even considered—braising a whole duck, but it really is a wonderful preparation. This broth is influenced by *bak kut teh*, a rich and meaty soup I tried in Singapore. An earlier version of this dish contained rice, but we found that the potatoes work better as the spices and braising liquid get soaked up in a much more satisfying way.

2 (2 1/2- to 3-pound) ducks

SHERRY MARINADE

8 cups dry sherry

1 tablespoon black peppercorns

2 cinnamon sticks

2 bay leaves

12 star anise

1 tablespoon fennel seeds

1/2 tablespoon cardamom seeds

1 head garlic, halved crosswise

1 (2- to 3-inch) piece of ginger, smashed

1/2 tablespoon coriander seeds

8 cups water, or enough to cover the ducks

1 cup diced onion

1/2 cup sliced carrots

1/2 cup sliced celery

1 tablespoon black peppercorns

2 bay leaves

8 cups Veal Stock (page 179) or Chicken Stock (page 177)

1 cup Cabernet Sauvignon or other dry red wine

3/4 cup mushroom soy sauce

3/4 cup mirin (sweet sake)

Salt and pepper to taste

4 stalks choy sum

1/4 cup butter

2 cups assorted mushrooms, such as oyster (sliced), shiitakes (quartered), morels (quartered), or button mushrooms (quartered)

1 tablespoon minced garlic

1 tablespoon minced shallots

4 cups Roasted Garlic Smashed Potatoes (page 137)

4 star anise, for garnish

4 cinnamon sticks, for garnish

12 chives, for garnish

Remove the wing tips and necks of the ducks and reserve for stock (see below). Place the ducks in a large, high-sided roasting pan.

To prepare the marinade, in a large bowl, combine the sherry, peppercorns, cinnamon, bay leaves, star anise, fennel, cardamom, garlic, ginger, coriander, and water. Pour over the ducks. Marinate in the refrigerator for 24 hours, turning the ducks occasionally.

Preheat the oven to 400°.

Place the reserved duck wing tips and necks in a roasting pan and roast in the oven for 25 to 30 minutes, or until golden brown.

In a bowl, combine the onion, carrots, celery, peppercorns, and bay leaves. Add to the duck wing tips and necks, and continue to roast about 25 minutes, or until they are brown and caramelized. Transfer to a stockpot. To the roasting pan, add 4 cups of the refrigerated marinade. Place over high heat on the stovetop for 8 to 10 minutes to deglaze and reduce to 2 cups. Add to the stockpot, scraping the pan. Add the stock and bring to a boil. Reduce the heat and simmer for 2 hours,

(continued)

(continued)

skimming any impurities that rise to the surface. Strain and reserve.

Meanwhile, reheat the oven to 325°. Remove the ducks from the marinade, pat dry, and roast for 1 1/2 to 2 hours, or until golden brown. Let cool slightly.

To prepare the braising liquid, in a saucepan over medium-high heat, reduce the wine by half. Add the mushroom soy sauce and mirin and continue to cook for 4 to 5 minutes, or until reduced by one quarter and thick and syrupy. Add the strained stock, bring to a boil and simmer for 30 minutes.

Increase the oven to 400°.

When the duck is cool, cut the breast meat from each duck in one piece. Cut off each leg in one piece and remove the thigh bone, leaving the drumstick intact. Transfer to a large casserole or roasting pan. Add the braising liquid, cover, and braise in the oven for about 2 hours, or until tender.

Remove the duck meat from the casserole and keep warm. Strain the braising liquid into a saucepan. Simmer the liquid for 15 to 20 minutes, skimming any impurities, and season with salt and pepper.

In a saucepan of boiling salted water, blanch the choy sum for 2 minutes. In a sauté pan over medium-high heat, melt the butter. Add the mushrooms and sauté for 2 to 3 minutes. Add the garlic and shallots and cook for about 1 minute longer, or until golden brown. Season with salt.

To serve, divide the potatoes among individual plates and shape in a flattened circle. Place the choy sum on the potatoes and top with half a duck breast and a leg. Spoon the mushroom mixture over and around the duck and garnish with the star anise, a cinnamon stick, and the chives. Spoon about 2 tablespoons of the braising liquid over the duck and around the potatoes.

YIELD: 4 SERVINGS

Chinatown Roasted Duck Risotto with Corn and Water Chestnuts

This is another recipe adapted from a traditional Chinese dish—Chinese duck stuffed with barley—that I enjoyed as a child in restaurants and at family gatherings. Look for Chinese roasted duck in local Chinese markets. In my version of this classic, I employ the Italian technique for risotto so that the rice has a creamy texture, then use Asian flavors rather than a lot of dairy ingredients that might mask the other delicate flavors. This dish is based on contrasting textures as well: the crunch of the corn and water chestnuts, the creamy risotto, the meaty duck, and the soft chickpeas.

$^1/_4$ cup dried chickpeas, soaked for 2 hours and drained

6 cups Five-Spice Risotto (page 138)

1 cup sliced Chinese roasted duck

$^1/_4$ cup fresh corn kernels (from $^1/_2$ ear corn)

$^1/_4$ cup diced fresh or canned water chestnuts

4 cups Five-Spice Broth (page 176)

$^1/_4$ cup grated Parmesan cheese

2 tablespoons butter

Lomi Tomato Relish (page 21)

8 sprigs cilantro, for garnish

$^1/_4$ cup Slivered Scallions (page 175), for garnish

Boil the chickpeas in salted water for 45 minutes to 1 hour, or until tender. Drain.

In a large saucepan over medium-high heat, combine the risotto, chickpeas, duck, corn, water chestnuts, and 2 cups of the broth. While stirring constantly, cook for about 4 minutes, or until the broth is absorbed by the rice. Swirl in the cheese and butter and cook, stirring, until melted.

Divide the risotto among individual bowls. Ladle $^1/_2$ cup of the remaining broth around the rice in each bowl. Top with the relish and garnish with the cilantro and scallions.

YIELD: 4 SERVINGS

Mungo Mango Lemongrass-Skewered Chicken with Mango Salsa and Tortilla Salad

This is a terrific summertime dish, created in the height of our mango season, to make use of the best mangoes in the world. Because of the seasonality, whenever I make this dish, I think of the old Mungo Jerry song, "In the Summertime," which explains the "Mungo Mango" of the recipe title. The very first time I ate a mango, I picked it from my Chinese grandfather's enormous backyard tree; some of my first memories of Hawaii after moving here from Japan when I was five are of his fruit orchard in full bloom. Picking his mangoes became my job, and I greatly enjoyed it as it meant I could eat as many mangoes as I liked! The sweet and spicy sauce also goes wonderfully well with pork and shrimp.

MANGO BARBECUE SAUCE

1 tablespoon vegetable oil
1/4 cup finely diced onion
1/2 tablespoon minced garlic
1/2 tablespoon chopped dried or canned chipotle chile
2 tablespoons sugar
1/4 cup balsamic vinegar
3/4 cup finely diced extra-ripe mango
1/4 cup diced tomato
1/8 teaspoon salt

MANGO VINAIGRETTE

1 cup diced extra-ripe mango
1/2 tablespoon freshly squeezed lime juice
Pinch of salt
2 teaspoons olive oil

TORTILLA SALAD

Vegetable oil for deep-frying
2 cups finely julienned corn tortillas
1/2 cup finely julienned red bell pepper
1/2 cup finely julienned yellow bell pepper
1/2 cup finely julienned green bell pepper
1 cup bean sprouts
1/2 cup cilantro leaves, large stems removed

1/2 cup thinly sliced scallions, green parts only, cut on a diagonal
1/4 cup Sambal Aioli (page 183)
Salt to taste

8 stalks lemongrass, outer leaves peeled
2 pounds boneless chicken breast, skin on
1/2 cup Balsamic Rum Syrup (page 39)
1 cup Mango Salsa (page 128)
4 basil sprigs
1/2 cup cilantro sprigs, for garnish

Prepare the grill.

To prepare the sauce, in a sauté pan over medium-high heat, heat the vegetable oil. Add the onion, garlic, and chipotle and sauté for 3 minutes. Add the sugar and balsamic vinegar and cook for 3 to 4 minutes, or until the liquid is thick and syrupy. Add the mango, tomato, and salt and cook, stirring occasionally, for 5 minutes. Transfer to a blender and purée until smooth.

To prepare the vinaigrette, in a blender, combine the mango, lime juice, and salt and purée until smooth. With the machine running, slowly add the oil until incorporated. Refrigerate until needed.

To prepare the tortilla salad, in a deep fryer or large saucepan, heat about 3 inches of vegetable oil to 350°. Deep-fry the tortilla strips for about 20 seconds, or until golden and crispy. Remove and drain on paper towels. In a bowl, combine the bell peppers, sprouts, cilantro, scallions, aioli, and tortilla strips. Season with salt. Refrigerate until needed.

Halve the lemongrass lengthwise and sharpen the ends to form skewers. Cut the chicken breast into 16 strips and thread onto the lemongrass skewers (skewers should be discarded after use and not eaten). Marinate in two thirds of the sauce for 5 minutes. Grill, basting the chicken periodically with the remaining sauce, for 5 to 7 minutes, or until cooked through.

To serve, arrange the salad in the center of individual plates. Place 4 of the skewers in a tepeelike design over the salad. Drizzle the vinaigrette and Balsamic Syrup around each salad. Place a small mound of salsa between each skewer. Top each teepee with a basil sprig. Garnish with the cilantro.

YIELD: 4 SERVINGS

Surf and Turf: Grilled Beef Tenderloin and Kona Lobster-Scallop Medallions with Truffle Yaki Sauce and Wasabi Smashed Potatoes

This is my elegant take on surf and turf, if I do say so myself. Combining meat and seafood may be something of a cliché, but it's still popular, and we enjoy coming up with new combinations at the restaurant. In this recipe I combine the flavors of truffles and soy, which makes an intriguing if unexpected partnership. ("Truffle Yaki" is a play on the word *teriyaki*, the Japanese soy sauce–based marinade.) This is also a dish of many diverse and unexpected flavors, such as the wasabi in the potatoes.

POTATOES

1 (8- to 10-ounce) baking potato, peeled
2 tablespoons vegetable oil
Salt and pepper to taste

ASPARAGUS

1/4 cup peanut oil
1/4 cup balsamic vinegar
Juice of 1 orange
1 teaspoon minced garlic
4 sprigs basil, bruised
24 thin asparagus spears, trimmed to 3 or 4 inches

MUSHROOMS

1 cup olive oil
2 teaspoons minced garlic
1 tablespoon minced shallots
4 sprigs thyme, chopped
1 cup oyster mushrooms

2 lobster tails, halved lengthwise
4 (2-ounce) scallops
4 (6-ounce) beef tenderloin medallions
Salt and pepper to taste
1/4 cup Green Butter (page 181)

TRUFFLE YAKI SAUCE

1/2 cup Soy Vinaigrette (page 90)
1/2 tablespoon cornstarch

1/2 tablespoon water
1 cup heavy cream
2 tablespoons truffle butter

4 sprigs chervil
3 cups Wasabi Smashed Potatoes (page 137)
12 Linguini Sticks (page 44)
4 sprigs tat soi or watercress
4 teaspoons Basil Oil (page 181)
1 teaspoon finely sliced chives

Preheat the oven to 350°.

Lightly rub the potato with the oil and season with salt and pepper. Place in a roasting pan and roast for about 1 hour, or until light golden brown and cooked through. Remove and let cool. Prepare the grill.

In a shallow bowl, combine the peanut oil, vinegar, orange juice, garlic, basil, and asparagus. Marinate for 10 minutes. In a separate bowl, combine the olive oil, garlic, shallots, thyme, and mushrooms. Marinate for 10 minutes.

Wrap each half lobster tail around a scallop and secure with a bamboo skewer. Season the beef with salt and pepper. Grill the beef for about 5 minutes on each side, or to the desired doneness. Grill the aspara-

gus and mushrooms for 4 to 5 minutes. Grill the seafood for 2 to 3 minutes on each side, basting occasionally with the Green Butter.

To prepare the sauce, in a saucepan, bring the vinaigrette to a boil, skimming off any impurities as they rise to the surface. In a cup, mix the cornstarch and water. Add to the vinaigrette and cook about 3 minutes, or until thickened. In another saucepan, over medium-high heat, reduce the cream by half. Stir in 1/4 cup of the thickened soy vinaigrette and the truffle butter. Keep warm.

Arrange the beef on individual plates. Top with the mushrooms and lobster-wrapped scallops. Garnish with the chervil. Cut off the ends of the roast potato and cut crosswise into 4 equal parts. Place the mashed potatoes in a pastry bag. Pipe the potatoes on top of each slice of roasted potato. Divide the potatoes and asparagus among the plates. Garnish the potatoes with the Linguini Sticks and a sprig of tat soi. Drizzle with the Truffle Yaki Sauce, Basil Oil, and the reserved 1/4 cup of thickened soy vinaigrette. Garnish with the chives.

YIELD: 4 SERVINGS

Braised Veal Shanks and Smashed Taro with Poi Sauce

Poi makes a flavorful thickener and works well with the many hearty flavors in this recipe. Poi stew—consisting of beef, vegetables, and a broth thickened with poi—is a local home cooked classic. In fact, I describe this dish as osso bucco meets poi stew.

1 pound celery, coarsely chopped

1 pound carrots, coarsely chopped

2 pounds onions, coarsely chopped

$1/2$ cup vegetable oil

4 (12- to 14-ounce) veal shanks

Salt and pepper to taste

$1^1/2$ cups red wine

8 cups Veal Stock (page 179)

2 bulbs garlic, halved crosswise

4 sprigs thyme

1 tablespoon peppercorns

3 bay leaves

2 tomatoes, halved

$1/4$ cup tomato paste

POI SAUCE

1 cup Veal Stock (page 179)

$1/2$ cup poi

Salt and pepper to taste

CORN AND MUSHROOMS

1 tablespoon olive oil

2 tablespoons thinly sliced mushrooms

2 tablespoons fresh corn kernels

4 teaspoons Green Butter (page 181)

Taro Smash (page 135)

Lomi Tomato Relish (page 21)

Poi Vinaigrette (page 8)

4 rosemary sprigs, for garnish

Preheat the oven to 400°.

In a large roasting pan, combine the celery, carrots, and onions. Add $1/4$ cup of the vegetable oil and toss to coat. Roast for about 30 minutes, or until golden brown and caramelized.

Season the veal with salt and pepper. In a large, heavy skillet or sauté pan over medium-high heat, heat the remaining $1/4$ cup of the vegetable oil. Brown the veal on all sides, adding a little more oil if necessary. Add to the roasting pan with the vegetables. Remove the excess oil from the skillet, add the red wine, and deglaze over high heat. Pour the wine and pan drippings into the roasting pan. Add the stock, garlic, thyme, peppercorns, bay leaves, tomatoes, and tomato paste and cover the pan with foil. Braise in the oven for 3 hours, or until the shanks are tender. Remove the shanks from the pan and strain the braising liquid, reserving 4 cups for the poi sauce.

To prepare the poi sauce, in a saucepan over medium-high heat, combine the reserved 4 cups of braising liquid, stock, and poi. Whisk together with a wire whisk until the sauce reaches a simmer; reduce the heat to medium-low and simmer for 30 minutes, skimming any impurities that rise to the surface. Season with salt and pepper and strain through a fine-mesh sieve before serving.

To prepare the corn and mushrooms, in a sauté pan over high heat, heat the olive oil. Add the mushrooms and sauté for about 3 minutes, or until golden brown. Stir in the corn and butter and cook for about 2 minutes longer, or until the butter melts.

To serve, place the Taro Smash in a pastry bag fitted with a star tip and pipe around the edge of individual plates. Place the veal shanks in the center of the plates and cover with the Poi Sauce. Spoon the corn and mushroom mixture on the shanks and top with the relish. Drizzle the vinaigrette around the shanks and vegetables. Garnish with a rosemary sprig.

YIELD: 4 SERVINGS

Poi, a paste made from taro root, is a Hawaiian staple that is often misunderstood. Sometimes, poi is deliberately left to ferment to give it a sour flavor. This makes it an acquired taste appreciated by the locals, but which often the uninitiated understandably leave to one side of their plate. Taro and poi were foundations of the diet of ancient Polynesians and Hawaiians.

Roasted Shiitake Mushrooms and Grilled Asparagus with Roasted Garlic Smashed Potatoes and Salsas

I created this recipe more by accident than design. When one of our guests requested a vegetarian entrée, I pulled together various components from that evening's menu to form this dish. It turned out so well that it's been a standby of mine ever since, and it has been on our menu at Alan Wong's from the day we opened. I know that vegetarian dishes are more in demand today than ever before, and as I learn more about this style of cooking, I hope to incorporate more into my menus. I enjoy the challenge of creating interesting, flavorful vegetarian recipes.

ASPARAGUS

$^1/_2$ cup peanut oil

$^1/_2$ cup balsamic vinegar

Juice of 1 orange

1 teaspoon minced garlic

8 sprigs basil, bruised

48 thin asparagus spears (trimmed to 3 or 4 inches)

MUSHROOMS

16 shiitake mushroom caps

Salt and pepper to taste

2 cloves garlic, thinly sliced

$^3/_4$ cup Basil Oil (page 181)

3 cups Roasted Garlic Smashed Potatoes (page 137)

$^1/_2$ cup Black Bean Salsa (page 129)

$^1/_2$ cup Fresh Corn Salsa (page 129)

$^1/_4$ cup Tomato–Chile Pepper Vinaigrette (page 58)

16 sprigs cilantro, for garnish

To prepare the asparagus, in a baking dish, combine the peanut oil, vinegar, orange juice, garlic, basil, and asparagus. Marinate for 4 hours.

Prepare the grill. Preheat the oven to 325°.

To prepare the mushrooms, place the shiitakes upside down in a roasting pan. Season with salt and pepper and top with the garlic. Drizzle the oil over the mushrooms. Roast for about 30 minutes, or until golden brown.

Grill the asparagus for 4 to 5 minutes, or until tender.

Place a 3-inch ring mold, 4 inches high, in the center of an individual plate. Using a pastry bag, pipe the potatoes into the mold and press down with the bottom of a glass or cup to compact. Top with 2 tablespoons of the bean salsa and again press down gently to compact. Carefully remove the mold. Arrange 12 asparagus spears with the stem ends touching the potato and the tips towards the edge of the plate. Arrange 4 mushroom caps between the asparagus and add the corn salsa. Drizzle the vinaigrette around the plate. Garnish the bean salsa with the cilantro. Repeat for the remaining servings.

YIELD: 4 SERVINGS

Grilled Lamb Chops with Macadamia-Coconut Crust, Star Anise Sauce, and Asian Ratatouille

This deliciously rich dish is inspired by the French classic, *carré d'agneau caramelisé*—caramelized rack of lamb—that was prepared at Lutèce in New York. I have introduced the exotic flavors of coconuts, macadamia nuts, and star anise to give it a distinctively Asian accent. I also wanted to create one lamb dish that would stop people from asking for mint jelly. I promise you, it won't be needed here!

COCONUT-GINGER CREAM

³/4 cup canned unsweetened coconut milk

1 tablespoon sugar

1 (1-inch) piece of ginger

STAR ANISE SAUCE

1¹/2 cups Five-Spice Broth (page 176)

2 star anise

4 tablespoons butter

2 tablespoons all-purpose flour

1¹/2 tablespoons mushroom soy sauce

3¹/2 cups Lamb Jus (page 178)

Salt and pepper to taste

COCONUT CRUST

¹/2 cup coconut flakes

¹/2 cup honey

2 tablespoons Dijon mustard

¹/2 tablespoon minced garlic

1 teaspoon minced fresh thyme

¹/2 tablespoon minced fresh flat-leaf parsley

¹/2 cup macadamia nuts, finely chopped

12 (2- to 3-ounce) lamb chops

4 cups Roasted Garlic Smashed Potatoes (page 137)

2 cups Asian Ratatouille (page 139)

4 sprigs rosemary

To prepare the cream, in a saucepan over medium-high heat, bring the coconut milk, sugar, and ginger to a boil. Reduce the heat to low and simmer, stirring frequently, about 3 or 4 minutes, or until the sauce thickens slightly. Continue to simmer for 10 minutes to let the flavors infuse. Strain into a clean pan and reheat just before serving.

Preheat the oven to 325°.

To prepare the Star Anise Sauce, in a saucepan, bring the broth and star anise to a boil. Cook for about 8 to 10 minutes to reduce by half. Meanwhile, in a small saucepan, melt 2 tablespoons of the butter and stir in the flour. Cook for 2 to 3 minutes, stirring, to form a roux. To the broth, add the mushroom soy sauce and simmer for 2 minutes. Add the lamb jus and roux and simmer for 30 minutes. Season with salt and pepper and swirl in the remaining 2 tablespoons of butter. Strain into a clean saucepan and reheat just before serving.

To prepare the crust, spread the coconut flakes on a cookie sheet and toast in the oven for 5 minutes, stirring occasionally. Let cool. In a bowl, combine the honey and mustard. Add the garlic, thyme, parsley, toasted coconut, and macadamia nuts.

Reheat the oven to 400°. Prepare the grill.

Grill the lamb chops for about 4 minutes on each side for medium-rare, or to the desired doneness. Place the chops in a roasting pan and top with the Coconut Crust. Finish in the oven for 2 to 3 minutes.

To serve, using a pastry bag, pipe the potatoes onto the center of individual plates. Pour the Star Anise Sauce around the potatoes. Lean 3 chops against the potatoes and place the ratatouille between the chops. Drizzle the Coconut-Ginger Cream over the Star Anise Sauce. Garnish the potatoes with a rosemary sprig.

YIELD: 4 SERVINGS

Kahua Ranch on the Big Island is our source of top-quality lamb, and owner Monte Richards is a wonderful individual and quite a character. He usually supplies us with one whole lamb carcass every week, and I enjoy teaching my staff about butchering and using all the parts, not just the more popular rack, legs, and loins. Some wonderfully flavorful dishes can be made with the neck and shoulder, for example.

Mixed Grill of Kahua Ranch Lamb: Pohaberry-Glazed Rack, Homemade Sausage, and Lamb Medallions

With three cuts of lamb, this dish is more labor-intensive than using just one, but the extra effort is well worth it. The curing salt—sodium nitrate—called for in the sausage recipe is necessary only if you are using casings to make links and curing the sausage in the refrigerator for a couple of days. It prevents the texture of the sausage from becoming too much like meat loaf. Do not use curing salt if you are making the mixture into patties. You can substitute a tart orange marmalade for the pohaberry preserves and fresh berries.

3 tomatoes, quartered

1 tablespoon olive oil

Salt and pepper to taste

LAMB SAUSAGE

1 tablespoon olive oil

1/4 cup minced onion

8 ounces coarsely ground lamb meat

4 ounces coarsely ground pork fat

1/2 teaspoon minced garlic

1/2 teaspoon minced fresh thyme

1/2 teaspoon cayenne

Salt and pepper to taste

Pinch of curing salt (optional)

Poha is the Hawaiian name given to the cape gooseberry, or lantern berry, which bears golden fruit covered in a lantern-shaped papery husk. In Hawaii, pohaberries are grown mostly on the Big Island.

POHABERRY GLAZE

1 cup pohaberry preserves

1 cup fresh pohaberries, diced

1 tablespoon Dijon mustard

1 tablespoon chopped fresh thyme leaves

1 tablespoon minced garlic

1 tablespoon minced fresh flat-leaf parsley

RACK AND LOIN OF LAMB

2 tablespoons olive oil

1 rack of lamb (4 double lamb chops)

Salt and pepper to taste

8 ounces lamb loin, cut into 4 medallions

1/4 cup haricots verts, trimmed

1 tablespoon butter

1/2 cup fresh corn kernels

3 cups Roasted Garlic Smashed Potatoes (page 137)

4 sprigs rosemary, for garnish

Preheat the oven to 300°. Prepare the grill.

Place the tomatoes in a roasting pan, drizzle with the olive oil, and season with salt and pepper. Roast for 30 to 35 minutes.

To prepare the lamb sausage, in a sauté pan over medium heat, heat the olive oil. Add the onion and sauté for 4 to 5 minutes. In a bowl, combine the cooked onions, ground lamb, ground pork fat, garlic, thyme, and cayenne. Season with salt and pepper. Form into 8 small patties. Grill the sausage for 3 to 4 minutes on each side, or until fully cooked.

Alternatively, use casings to make links. Rinse the casings out before use. Add the curing salt to the sausage and mix well. Stuff the casings and air-dry the stuffed sausages in the refrigerator for at least 1 day and up to 2 days before using. Sauté the sausage in 1 tablespoon vegetable oil.

To prepare the glaze, in a stainless steel or glass bowl, combine the pohaberry preserves, pohaberries, mustard, thyme, garlic, and parsley and mix well using a wire whisk.

To prepare the rack and loin, in a sauté pan over high heat, heat the olive oil. Season the lamb rack with salt and pepper. Sear until browned on all sides. Transfer to the grill and cook for 2 minutes on each side. Brush on the glaze as you would a barbecue sauce and grill for another 2 to 3 minutes on each side for medium rare, or to the desired doneness. Meanwhile, season the lamb loin with salt and pepper. Sear in the sauté pan until browned on all sides. Grill for 3 to 4 minutes on each side, or to the desired doneness.

In a saucepan of boiling salted water, blanch the haricots verts for 1 minute. In a sauté pan over medium-high heat, melt the butter. Add the corn and haricots verts and sauté for 2 to 3 minutes, or until tender.

Cut the sausages (if using links) into slices, the rack into 8 chops, and the loin into 4 slices.

Divide the haricots verts and corn among individual plates. Using a pastry bag, pipe the potatoes on top of the vegetables. Arrange the chops, loin, and sausage around the vegetables. Place a roasted tomato quarter between each serving of lamb (3 quarters per plate). Garnish the potato with an upright rosemary sprig.

YIELD: 4 SERVINGS

Hawaiian Petroglyphs

Petroglyphs (a word derived from the Greek for "stone carving") are aesthetic symbols etched into rocks dating from prehistoric times, and they can be found in most parts of the world. The design of this book incorporates reproductions of Hawaiian petroglyphs (called *kaha ki'i*), which likewise date from ancient times—several centuries before first Western contact.

These enigmatic and inventive petroglyph symbols are most commonly found in open terrain in dry areas, typically near trails between settlements rather than in them. They are usually placed in clusters, often carved into smooth lava fields, and the most notable concentration of petroglyphs are found on the Big Island of Hawaii. Most seem to have been created by pounding or carving with stone implements.

Some experts believe that the symbols were records of trips made or of historical events and legends; others think they were formed by priests and held spiritual significance; still others hold that they were protective images created to ensure good health and long life. Among the principal images of Hawaiian petroglyphs are human figures, canoes, sails and paddles, domestic animals, tools, and godlike representations.

Hawaiian petroglyphs are evocative and popular designs that are reproduced today everywhere on the islands, from business logos to colorful aloha shirts to contemporary artwork.

Pork Tenderloin Medallions with Gingered Sweet Potatoes and Pineapple–Macadamia Nut Relish

Back in the unenlightened days of the 1960s and '70s, the saying went that the best meal you'd get on your Hawaiian vacation was the meal coming over on the plane. In culinary terms, Hawaii was known then for mahi mahi sprinkled with macadamia nuts, and Ham Steak Aloha—grilled ham steak with a canned pineapple ring smothered in a gooey sweet sauce and, if you were really lucky, a maraschino cherry garnish. We've come a long way since those days. Actually, pork matched with the flavors of fruit is a classic combination in many cuisines. Pork and apple sauce is probably the best-known and most traditional pairing, but pears and prunes also complement the sweet tones of the meat. This is my updated tropical twist on pork and pineapple.

CRISPY PLANTAIN CHIPS

1 green plantain

Vegetable oil for deep-frying

$^1/_4$ cup vegetable oil

2 pounds pork tenderloin, silver skin removed, cut into 16 medallions

Salt and pepper to taste

Gingered Sweet Potatoes (page 16)

1 cup Pineapple–Macadamia Nut Relish (page 132)

$^1/_2$ cup Pineapple Vinaigrette (page 39)

$^1/_4$ cup Basil Oil (page 181)

$^1/_4$ cup Balsamic Rum Syrup (page 39)

4 sprigs culantro, for garnish

To prepare the chips, peel the plantain, using a knife if necessary. Using a mandolin slicer, cut the plantain lengthwise into 12 very thin strips. In a deep fryer or large saucepan over high heat, heat 3 inches of vegetable oil to 350°. Deep-fry the plantain for 3 to 4 minutes, or until golden brown and crisp. Remove and drain on paper towels.

In a heavy sauté pan or skillet over medium-high heat, heat the $^1/_4$ cup vegetable oil. Season the pork with salt and pepper. Sauté for 4 to 5 minutes on each side, or until cooked through.

To serve, using a pastry bag, pipe the potatoes onto the center of individual plates. Arrange 4 pork medallions on each plate, spaced evenly around the potatoes. Top the pork with the relish and drizzle the vinaigrette, Basil Oil, and Balsamic Rum Syrup around the potatoes and pork. Garnish each seving with 3 of the plantain chips, sticking upright in the potatoes, and a sprig of culantro.

YIELD: 4 SERVINGS

Sides and Condiments

Sides and Condiments

The recipes in this chapter are side dishes that you can serve as accompaniments to your own recipes and as integral components of many recipes elsewhere in this book. I have always enjoyed the Asian style of eating where several elements and flavors are gathered on the same plate. Growing up, home cooking was never as simple as the then-standard protein, starch, and a vegetable. Instead, all kinds of interesting items shared our table, each one designed to complement the foundation of the meal: rice. There were hot pickles, salty pickles, pickled cucumbers, pickled cabbage, pickled eggplant, kim chee, and various other Japanese, Chinese, Filipino, and Korean condiments. The combinations were endless, and each element had many different uses. Most of the recipes in this chapter are designed with this philosophy in mind.

In cooking school, I was taught the classic sauces, but as my cooking style developed, I found that I preferred fresh salsas, relishes, chutneys, and vinaigrettes over heavy dairy-based sauces of European influence. There are exceptions to this rule, but I find that the flavor, texture, and color of these fresh foods make a bold and exciting statement, stimulate the eye, and add zip to the palate. They make other foods seem more alive, and the raw or lightly cooked ingredients they contain are straightforward, simple, and healthful.

These recipes typify my belief that cooking involves four simple elements: correct seasoning, balance of fats and acids, proper technique, and a passion for the freshest quality ingredients. Experiment by pairing these recipes with different dishes and in different combinations with each other. Most of all, have fun with them.

Every chef has his or her own rules and interpretation, but here are my definitions about the distinction between salsas, relishes, and chutneys. Our salsas are made with raw ingredients and usually contain some kind of heat, such as chiles. Typically, they also contain oil, acid, cilantro, and scallions. Relishes are usually savory, whereas chutneys are sweet in flavor, either through the addition of sugar or naturally from the fruit.

Alan's Asian Guacamole

There was a time when I didn't have a clue about guacamole. I rarely ate Mexican food growing up. One afternoon, my sister brought some shrimp over to grill, and I decided to make a side dish from the avocados that grew in our backyard and ingredients that were in the kitchen. I added many of the items in this recipe, and it turned out really well. Only later I realized I'd made an Asian version of classic Mexican guacamole. It's been a standby of mine as long as I've cooked professionally.

2 avocados, peeled, pitted, and diced

1/2 cup diced onion

1/2 cup diced tomato

3 tablespoons sake

1/4 cup sliced scallions, green part only

2 tablespoons freshly squeezed lime juice

2 tablespoons minced ginger

1 tablespoon chopped cilantro

1 tablespoon vegetable oil

1/2 teaspoon chile sauce with garlic (such as Sambal Oelek)

1 teaspoon Chile Pepper Water (page 175)

1 teaspoon salt

In a bowl, combine the avocados, onion, tomato, sake, scallions, lime juice, ginger, cilantro, oil, chile sauce, Chile Pepper Water, and salt. Mix gently without mashing the avocado. Serve immediately, or cover with plastic wrap and refrigerate for up to 2 days.

YIELD: 4 TO 5 CUPS

Mango Salsa

Although I use this salsa most often with chicken, it also works very well with tuna and most other fish. The clear sweetness of the mangoes and the subtle heat of the salsa make a classic combination. The key is to use ripe fruit. Of course, it helps to have the best mangoes in the world to work with as we do here in Hawaii. My favorite varieties of mango are Pirie and Hayden.

1/2 cup finely diced mango

1/4 cup finely diced tomato

1/4 cup finely diced scallions, green parts only

2 tablespoons finely diced red onion

1 teaspoon minced ginger

1 teaspoon minced cilantro

1 red Hawaiian chile, or 1/2 red serrano chile, minced

1 teaspoon freshly squeezed lime juice

1 teaspoon olive oil

Salt to taste

In a bowl, thoroughly combine the mango, tomato, scallions, onion, ginger, cilantro, chile, lime juice, and oil. Season with salt. Refrigerate for up to 24 hours.

YIELD: 1 CUP

Black Bean Salsa

I have always liked beans of all kinds. While I was living on the Big Island, I had a vegetarian roommate, which gave me the opportunity to eat a lot of beans. As I began learning more about food, I got to appreciate beans all the more for the important role they play in a healthful diet. Black beans are a common feature of Central and South American cooking, but this salsa goes with almost every kind of food.

1 cup cooked black beans

1/2 cup diced tomatoes

2 tablespoons sliced scallions, green parts only

2 tablespoons finely diced red onion

1 tablespoon chopped cilantro

3 tablespoons olive oil

1 teaspoon freshly squeezed lime juice

1/2 tablespoon minced garlic

1 red Hawaiian chile, or 1/2 red serrano chile, minced

1 teaspoon Chile Pepper Water (page 175)

Salt to taste

In a bowl, thoroughly combine the beans, tomatoes, scallions, onion, cilantro, oil, lime juice, garlic, chile, and Chile Pepper Water. Season with salt. Keep refrigerated for up to 24 hours and serve at room temperature.

YIELD: 2 CUPS

Fresh Corn Salsa

Growing up in Wahiawa on Oahu, the North Shore—surf capital of the world—was my backyard. On the way to search for bodysurfing waves, my friends and I would pass large cornfields in Kahuku. Sometimes, we would stop at the roadside stands selling incredibly sweet and tender corn and eat it there and then: peeling back the leaves and eating it raw. These vivid memories of taste and texture often come back when I taste corn, especially the local variety.

1 1/2 cups fresh corn kernels (from 2 or 3 ears corn)

2 tablespoons sliced scallions, green parts only

2 tablespoons finely diced red onion

2 tablespoons finely diced red bell pepper

1 tablespoon chopped cilantro

1/2 teaspoon minced garlic

2 tablespoons olive oil

1 teaspoon rice vinegar

1/2 teaspoon chile paste with garlic (such as Sambal Oelek)

Salt to taste

In a saucepan of boiling salted water, blanch the corn for 2 minutes. Drain and transfer to an ice bath to cool. In a bowl, thoroughly combine the corn, scallions, onion, bell pepper, cilantro, garlic, oil, vinegar, and chile paste. Season with salt. Serve at room temperature.

YIELD: 2 CUPS

Papaya–Red Onion Salsa

Papaya is a fruit you grow up with in Hawaii, like mango and pineapple, especially if you have a tree in your backyard as we did. My favorite type is the strawberry papaya (especially those grown on Kauai) with a pink flesh and deep melonlike flavor. Papaya is a very versatile fruit that can be used green (in its unripe form) in Southeast Asian–style salads or added to cooked soups and stews. This salsa accompanies Kalbi Short Rib Tacos (page 43) and is good with any pork dish and most fish and shellfish. Be careful when using papaya, as its aroma and flavor can overwhelm other ingredients or food it's served with. The solution is simple: cut the flavor of the fruit with citrus juice such as lime or lemon.

1 cup finely diced ripe papaya

1/4 cup finely diced red onion

1 tablespoon chopped cilantro

2 tablespoons finely diced red bell pepper

3 red Hawaiian chiles, or 1 small red serrano or red Thai chile, minced

1/2 teaspoon minced garlic

2 tablespoons julienned scallions, green parts only

1 tablespoon freshly squeezed lime juice

In a bowl, thoroughly combine the papaya, onion, cilantro, bell pepper, chiles, garlic, scallions, and lime juice. This salsa is best used the same day.

YIELD: 1 1/2 CUPS

Thai Cucumber Salsa

This salsa's crunchy texture is similar to Japanese *namasu*, but this dish is not sweet-and-sour in flavor like that classic. Instead, the fish sauce, chiles, and tamarind give it a Thai-style complexity that goes very well with most fish.

1 cup thinly sliced Japanese or hothouse cucumber

1 teaspoon salt

1/4 cup diced red bell pepper

2 pieces lemongrass, trimmed to the bottom 6 inches and bruised

4 kaffir lime leaves, bruised

4 or 5 cilantro sprigs, bruised

Juice of 1/2 lemon

2 tablespoons olive oil

1 tablespoon Thai fish sauce

1 tablespoon tamarind paste

1/2 teaspoon Thai chile sauce (such as Sriracha or Golden Mountain)

In a bowl, combine the cucumber and salt. Let sit at room temperature for 4 to 5 hours, or in the refrigerator overnight. Rinse off the salt with cold water and drain off all excess water. Transfer to a mixing bowl and add the bell pepper, lemongrass, lime leaves, cilantro, lemon juice, oil, fish sauce, tamarind, and chile sauce. Remove and discard the lemongrass and lime leaves before serving.

YIELD: 1 3/4 CUPS

Fresh Water Chestnut Salsa

As the name suggests, water chestnuts are edible tubers of a water plant, typically cultivated in flooded rice paddies in their native China. They are not related to chestnuts at all, although the shells look similar. Once you try fresh water chestnuts, with their delicious sweetness and crunch, you'll agree that the hunt for them is worth the effort. The best bet for finding fresh water chestnuts is an Asian market. Failing that, use canned or jicama instead. This salsa is best fresh, but it will keep for 2 days if refrigerated.

1 cup finely diced tomatoes

2 $1/2$ tablespoons finely diced onion

2 $1/2$ tablespoons finely sliced scallions, mostly green and some of the white parts

2 tablespoons peeled and diced fresh or canned water chestnuts

1 tablespoon minced cilantro

1 $1/2$ tablespoons Chile Pepper Water (page 175)

Salt to taste

In a bowl, thoroughly combine the tomatoes, onion, scallions, water chestnuts, cilantro, and Chile Pepper Water. Season with salt. Refrigerate until needed. Serve chilled.

YIELD: 1 $1/2$ CUPS

Tomato-Ginger Relish

I grew up with tomato salads—my Filipino stepfather loved them, and my mother almost always made one for dinner. Her tomato salads usually contained flavors from his homeland, such as ginger, garlic, fish sauce, and soy sauce, sometimes accompanied with sweet potato leaves or other greens and vegetables. This versatile relish, which plays on Mom's recipe, accompanies the Nori-Wrapped Tempura Bigeye Tuna (page 53), and it also works well with any grilled meat or fish. It should be eaten the day that it's made.

1 cup diced tomato

$1/2$ tablespoon Ginger-Scallion Oil (page 180)

2 tablespoons sliced scallions, green parts only

2 tablespoons minced sweet Maui onion

1 teaspoon black sesame seeds

1 teaspoon white sesame seeds, toasted

$1/2$ tablespoon mirin

$1/2$ tablespoon rice wine vinegar

3 drops Thai fish sauce

Salt to taste

In a bowl, thoroughly combine the tomato, oil, scallions, onion, sesame seeds, mirin, vinegar, and fish sauce. Season with salt. Refrigerate until needed.

YIELD: 1 $1/4$ CUPS

Mediterranean Relish

This relish contains European ingredients—capers, olives, and anchovies—that I was never exposed to growing up in an Asian household. Once I began to travel, and I discovered these flavors, I was particularly intrigued by how they could be combined with Asian ingredients. I use this colorful combination with "Stacked" Eggplant and Puna Goat Cheese Salad (page 77), but I also enjoy it with steak, poultry, and most fish. The relish is best eaten the day it is prepared.

¹/₂ cup diced tomato

1¹/₂ tablespoons diced onion

¹/₂ tablespoon rinsed diced capers

¹/₂ tablespoon chopped fresh basil leaves

2 tablespoons pitted and chopped Niçoise olives

2 anchovy fillets, minced

¹/₂ tablespoon minced garlic

2 teaspoons olive oil

¹/₂ teaspoon salt

In a bowl, thoroughly combine the tomato, onion, capers, basil, olives, anchovies, garlic, oil, and salt. Refrigerate until needed. Serve chilled.

YIELD: ³/₄ CUP

Pineapple–Macadamia Nut Relish

Macadamia nuts give this relish an interesting texture, and the complex fruity flavors are great with Pork Tenderloin (page 122), as well as chicken, tuna, swordfish, or other robustly flavored grilled fish. It's best eaten the same day it's made.

1 cup finely diced pineapple

¹/₂ cup finely diced mango

2 tablespoons finely peeled and diced fresh or canned water chestnuts

2 tablespoons finely diced macadamia nuts, toasted

1 tablespoon chopped fresh flat-leaf parsley

¹/₄ cup olive oil

1 tablespoon balsamic vinegar

Salt to taste

In a bowl, gently mix the pineapple, mango, water chestnuts, macadamia nuts, parsley, oil, and vinegar. Season with salt. Refrigerate until needed. Serve chilled.

YIELD: 2 CUPS

Minted Mango Relish

This bright, sweet-and-savory relish has a dash of heat to delight and tantalize the palate. I serve it with Kalua Turkey Quesadillas (page 11), but it makes a wonderful condiment with almost any fish or poultry dish.

$^1/_2$ cup finely diced mango

$^1/_2$ cup finely diced tomato

2 tablespoons finely sliced scallions, green parts only

1 teaspoon finely diced red onion

$^1/_4$ teaspoon minced red Hawaiian chile or red serrano chile

1 teaspoon chopped fresh mint

2 teaspoons freshly squeezed lime juice

Salt to taste

In a bowl, gently mix the mango, tomato, scallions, onion, chile, mint, and lime juice. Season with salt. Refrigerate until needed. Serve chilled.

YIELD: 1 CUP

The luscious, perfumed mango is native to India, where the tree is held sacred. From there, the fruit gradually spread throughout Southeast Asia until 1824, when Captain John Meek of Honolulu brought some mango seedlings home from the Philippines. These are believed to be the first mango trees grown in Hawaii. Along with the popular fruit, the large, prolific, and handsome trees also provide welcome shade to many a local backyard.

Li Hing Mui Chutney

Mention *li hing mui* to a local and watch them salivate. Just as many children on the mainland grow up on Cracker-Jack, here in Hawaii it's *li hing mui*, crack seed (see page 39). This chutney is a take on the Hawaiian specialty. I serve it most often with foie gras (page 39). It also goes wonderfully with pork and—believe it or not—vanilla ice cream. Store the chutney in the refrigerator for up to 3 days.

$^1/_4$ cup balsamic vinegar

$^1/_4$ cup sugar

1 teaspoon li hing mui powder

Juice of 1 lemon

1 cinnamon stick

$^1/_2$ cup diced dried pitted prunes

$^1/_2$ cup diced dried pitted apricots

$^1/_4$ cup diced bananas

$^1/_4$ cup diced macadamia nuts

$^1/_4$ cup diced pineapple

In a saucepan, bring the vinegar and sugar to a boil. Boil for 3 to 4 minutes, or until the mixture thickens to a syrup. Stir in the li hing mui, lemon juice, and cinnamon. Add the prunes and apricots, and cook for 1 minute longer. When cool, stir in the bananas, macadamia nuts, and pineapple.

YIELD: 2 CUPS

Basil–Macadamia Nut Pesto

In this delicious Hawaiian version of the Italian basil pesto, macadamia nuts replace pine nuts, Jack cheese replaces Parmesan, and I've added spinach leaves to the basil greens. Altogether, it goes well with the Asian flavors of many recipes throughout this book.

2 anchovy fillets, diced

1/4 cup chopped toasted
   macadamia nuts

1/2 cup grated Monterey Jack cheese

1/2 cup firmly packed spinach

1 cup firmly packed fresh basil

1/2 tablespoon minced garlic

Salt to taste

1/4 cup olive oil

In a blender, combine the anchovies, nuts, cheese, spinach, basil, and garlic. Season with salt. Purée until smooth. With the machine running, slowly add the oil until thoroughly incorporated. Refrigerate in an airtight container until needed.

YIELD: 2 CUPS

Because of the extensive plantations here and their popularity as a tourist souvenir, macadamia nuts are closely identified with Hawaii. However, the tree is native to the tropical rainforests of Australia. A prominent Scottish-born scientist living in Melbourne, John Macadam, first recognized the nuts' edible quality (although another type of macadamia tree bears bitter and inedible nuts). As a result, the pair of botanists who scientifically identified the tree named it after him. The first macadamia nuts were brought to Hawaii by a sugar plantation owner, William Purvis, around 1880, for growing as impressive ornamental trees. It was only in the 1920s that commercial orchards were planted with trees bearing the edible nuts. Since then, the Hawaiian macadamia nut industry has become one of the islands' most important.

Black Olive Tapenade

Growing up in Hawaii, I was aware of only one kind of olive: the sliced, canned version that topped pizzas. Today, you can buy a wide range of olives from California, Italy, Spain, France, and Greece. Some are packed in oil, others in brine. This recipe is a classic black olive tapenade. Sometimes, you just can't improve on a classic.

4 anchovy fillets, diced

1 tablespoon capers, rinsed and drained

$1/2$ cup pitted black Niçoise olives packed in oil

2 tablespoons olive oil

4 cloves garlic

In a blender, combine the anchovies, capers, olives, oil, and garlic. Purée until mostly smooth but still a little textured. Refrigerate until needed.

YIELD: $3/4$ CUP

Taro Smash

Taro sold in markets usually ranges from 8 ounces to 2 pounds. It has a brown, rough skin with a creamy flesh. There are many different kinds of taro, each typically tinged with gray, pink, or purple. Wetland taro makes the best poi (see page 116) and produces the best luau leaves. Smaller dryland (or Chinese) taro is crisper and is favored for taro chips. Use any kind of taro for this recipe. Taro is prepared many ways: boiled, as in this recipe, roasted, baked, fried, or deep-fried. Taro also is ground to make flour.

1 pound taro, peeled and cubed

8 ounces russet potato, peeled and cubed

$1/4$ cup butter, at room temperature

$1/3$ cup heavy cream, warmed

Salt to taste

Place the taro and potatoes in a steamer or vegetable basket set in a saucepan of lightly boiling water. Cover and steam for 45 minutes to 1 hour, or until soft. Drain and mash. Using a wire whisk, beat in the butter and warm cream. Whisk rapidly so the potato absorbs the other ingredients well. The consistency should be light and fluffy. Season with salt.

YIELD: 4 TO 5 CUPS

It is important to always cook taro thoroughly because in its raw state, or even partly cooked, taro has a mildly toxic acidity, caused by calcium chloride crystals, that irritates the lining of the mouth and throat.

Steamed White Rice

There's a saying in Hawaii, "any meal without rice is really just a snack." Growing up, I had rice for breakfast, lunch, and dinner, and enjoyed *musubi*, or rice balls, as an after-school snack. My mom still occasionally brings me a rice dish she's made for lunch. Short-grain Japanese-style rice is more prevalent in Hawaii than long grain, partly because its sticky consistency makes it so much easier to eat with chopsticks. At Alan Wong's, we serve both white "sticky" rice and brown rice.

2 cups short-grain white rice

2 cups water

Place the rice and water in a rice steamer, cover, and cook for 30 minutes. Remove and fluff the rice with a spoon before serving. Alternatively, place the rice and water in a saucepan and bring to a boil. Reduce the heat to a simmer, cover, and cook for 10 minutes, or until the water evaporates. Fluff before serving.

YIELD: ABOUT 4 CUPS

Rice is an important part of Hawaiian cuisine for historical and ethnic reasons. In the 1850s and 1860s, the earliest sugar plantation contract workers came from Asian countries such as China and Japan, and they brought rice with them. Early in the twentieth century, Filipinos, Koreans, and other Asian groups followed to work the pineapple plantations. Today, over half of the population of the state claims Asian heritage. Little wonder, then, that "two scoops rice" is the local term for the typical Hawaiian plate lunch.

Wasabi Smashed Potatoes

Wasabi is also called the Japanese horseradish and is used in similar ways. I partner it with beef dishes that have Asian accents like my Surf and Turf main course (page 115). These potatoes also make a great accompaniment with tuna steak. Adding the wasabi just before serving keeps the wasabi at maximum pungency.

¹/₄ cup grated fresh wasabi, or
 ¹/₂ cup wasabi paste
Roasted Garlic Smashed Potatoes
 (this page)

In a bowl, using a wire whisk, beat the wasabi into the potatoes just before serving.

YIELD: 4 TO 5 CUPS

If fresh wasabi is unavailable, use wasabi powder to make a paste. Use hot water to mix with the powder as this will release more of the wasabi's pungent qualities. Add only enough water so that when mixed in a cup or bowl, the paste will not come out if turned upside down. If not using immediately, keep the cup or bowl containing the wasabi inverted over a flat work surface or plate so the pungent fumes are enclosed for as long as possible and do not escape or evaporate. One final piece of advice: keep passing children and pets well back!

Roasted Garlic Smashed Potatoes

This is a classic and ever-popular mashed potato recipe, with the addition of roasted garlic. If you like, you can season the mashed potatoes with a little shichimi, cayenne, or other chile powder.

1 ¹/₂ pounds russet potatoes, peeled
 and cubed
2 heads Roasted Garlic (page 175)
¹/₂ cup butter, at room temperature
³/₄ cup heavy cream, warmed
Salt to taste

In a saucepan of boiling salted water, boil the potatoes for 15 to 20 minutes, or until soft. In a bowl, combine the potatoes and garlic. Using a wire whisk, beat in the butter and warm cream. Whisk rapidly, so the potato absorbs the other ingredients well. Season with salt.

YIELD: 4 TO 5 CUPS

Five-Spice Risotto

Risottos are one of my favorite comfort foods. They remind me of the Asian rice porridge *congee* (also called *jook* in China and *okayu* in Japan) that forms the base for other flavors and ingredients. Arborio rice, grown in Italy, is a short-grain rice with a high starch content, which gives it an attractively creamy texture. This risotto accompanies the Chinatown Roasted Duck (page 111) and is equally good as a starter.

5 cups Five-Spice Broth (page 176)

4 tablespoons olive oil

1¹/₂ cups quartered shiitake mushrooms

1 tablespoon minced garlic

¹/₂ diced onion

1 (2-inch) piece ginger, smashed

2 cups Arborio rice

¹/₄ cup white wine

Salt to taste

In a saucepan, bring the broth to a boil. Meanwhile, in a sauté pan over medium-high heat, heat 1 tablespoon of the olive oil. Add the mushrooms and sauté for 4 to 5 minutes, or until tender and golden brown. Remove the mushrooms and set aside.

Add the remaining 3 tablespoons of oil to the pan. Add the garlic and onion and sauté for 2 minutes. Add the ginger and rice, stirring so the rice is evenly coated with the oil.

Add the wine. Stirring constantly, add the hot broth, 1 cup at a time, letting the rice absorb the liquid before adding more. After the last addition, cook for 3 minutes longer. Total cooking time from the first addition of the broth should be about 12 minutes. Season with salt and mix in the mushrooms.

YIELD: 6 CUPS

Asian Ratatouille

This recipe is inspired by a Filipino dish, *pinacbet*. It adapts the classic Provençale vegetable stew with the addition of Asian ingredients. Like the traditional ratatouille, the longer you cook this recipe, the more color you will lose, so keep the cooking time to a minimum.

4 tablespoons olive oil

1 cup diced yellow squash

1 cup diced eggplant

1 cup diced zucchini

1 cup diced onion

1/4 cup diced red bell pepper

1/4 cup diced yellow bell pepper

1/4 cup diced green bell pepper

2 teaspoons minced garlic

2 teaspoons minced ginger

1 tablespoon Yamasa soy sauce or other brand

1 tablespoon oyster sauce

1 teaspoon sesame oil

1 teaspoon Thai fish sauce

1 cup diced tomato

In a wok or sauté pan over medium-high heat, heat 2 tablespoons of the olive oil. Add the squash, eggplant, zucchini, onion, and bell peppers and sauté for about 8 minutes, or until tender. Move the vegetables aside, add the remaining 2 tablespoons of olive oil, and heat through. Add the garlic and ginger to the center of the wok or pan and cook for 2 minutes, or until lightly brown. Add the soy sauce, oyster sauce, sesame oil, and fish sauce and cook for 2 minutes longer. Add the tomato and cook for 2 minutes more. Serve warm.

YIELD: 4 CUPS

Shrimp Hash

I use this tasty hash to stuff Steamed Moi (page 92), but it also makes a delicious filling for wontons or shiu mai. Like any hash, you can also serve it for brunch with eggs or a salad. Shape the hash into patties and sauté for 4 to 5 minutes on each side, or until golden brown. Grind the seafood in a meat grinder or food processor.

1/2 cup ground scallops plus 1/2 cup minced

1/2 cup ground shrimp plus 1/2 cup minced

1/4 cup finely diced shiitake mushrooms

6 tablespoons diced fresh or canned waterchestnuts

1/2 cup sliced scallions, mostly green and some white parts

3 tablespoons oyster sauce

2 teaspoons dark sesame oil

2 teaspoons chopped cilantro

2 teaspoons minced garlic

1 egg, beaten

In a bowl, thoroughly mix the scallops, shrimp, mushrooms, water chestnuts, scallions, oyster sauce, sesame oil, cilantro, garlic, and egg. Refrigerate until needed, but serve the same day.

YIELD: ABOUT 3 CUPS

Desserts

Desserts

Desserts provide a lasting impression, making them a very important part of any meal. As a chef, or as a home cook, you want your guests to end their meal on a high note and, hopefully, with a bang. I like my desserts to be fun, creative, colorful, and refreshing.

Hawaii has such a wonderful bounty of fresh tropical fruit and other high-quality ingredients that it would be wasteful not to use them. When we were in the process of planning the dessert menu at Alan Wong's, we began by listing the local ingredients we considered indispensable. As a result, the recipes that follow feature the rich, luscious flavors of pineapple, coconut, macadamia nuts, Hawaiian chocolate, mango, lychee, guava, passion fruit, Big Island Ka'u orange, Waimea strawberries, and star fruit. Some of our regular customers even bring in their prime backyard fruit and proudly ask us to use it in a dessert.

I like to serve desserts that are consistent with the rest of the meal in terms of style, texture, and balance of ingredients and flavors. Many of these desserts mirror the themes of earlier chapters by giving a contemporary or tropical twist to classics. This is the inspiration behind desserts such as the Baked Hawaii, our brûlées, and the Okinawan Sweet Potato Cheesecake. As a glance at the recipes that follow

Serving 100 percent Hawaiian-grown coffee with desserts that have been inspired by the flavors of paradise makes a nice touch. At Alan Wong's, we offer a variety of local coffees to accompany dessert. Most of the excellent coffee produced in the state comes from Kona on the Big Island, and our guests have a choice of estate-grown varieties, each with its own slightly different nuances in flavor. We also offer Kauai and Maui coffee that we have tasted and enjoyed. It's fun to see guests at a large table ordering all of the coffees and taste-testing them! We recommend brewing the coffee in French presses, like we do at the restaurant, as they preserve flavor and freshness better than other methods.

will tell you, some of our favorite desserts are sorbets and ice creams, and the flavors of the islands are perfectly suited for these too.

Much of the credit for these dessert recipes goes to Mark Okumura, who was born and raised in Honolulu. We met in culinary school at Kapiolani Community College, and he has been with us since the restaurant opened. He chose to be a chef for the best of reasons—he enjoys eating—and he was drawn to desserts from the very beginning. Because he grew up here, Mark has a special gift for understanding how to please our guests' palates. Hawaiians love sweets (people living in warm climates generally have a more pronounced sweet tooth than those in cooler climates), and Mark delivers. Mark's assistants, Mark Silva and Abigail Langlas, are also important players in the constantly evolving creative process taking place in the restaurant's pastry kitchen. Their work is also included in this chapter.

Hawaiian Vintage Chocolate Crunch Bars

Mark Okumura came up with this light and crunchy chocolate dessert with an interesting, soft texture that melts in the mouth. The gaufrette cookies are the thin, crispy wafers that are typically served with ice cream.

1 cup diced macadamia nuts

$1/4$ cup water

1 cup brown sugar

$1/2$ cup corn syrup

$1/4$ cup butter

$1/2$ teaspoon vanilla extract

1 teaspoon baking soda, sifted

$1/4$ cup macadamia nut oil, or vegetable oil

12 ounces gaufrette cookies (about 50)

$1 1/2$ pounds Hawaiian Vintage milk chocolate

$1 1/4$ pounds Hawaiian Vintage dark chocolate

$2 1/2$ cups heavy whipping cream

4 teaspoons macadamia nut liqueur

$1/4$ cup cocoa powder, for dusting

ANGLAISE

4 egg yolks

$1/4$ cup sugar

1 cup milk

1 vanilla bean, halved lengthwise and seeds scraped

CHOCOLATE SAUCE

4 ounces Hawaiian Vintage dark chocolate

$1/4$ cup heavy whipping cream

1 cup raspberries or other fresh fruit, for garnish

Preheat the oven to 250°. Grease a baking sheet and spatula. Line a 9-by-13-inch pan with plastic wrap.

Place the nuts on an ungreased baking sheet and toast for 10 minutes. In a heavy-bottomed saucepan over medium-high heat, combine the water, sugar, corn syrup, and butter. Heat until the mixture reaches 280° on a candy thermometer. Add the vanilla and toasted nuts. Carefully stir in the baking soda—use caution as the mixture will bubble up. Immediately pour onto the greased cookie sheet and spread evenly with the greased spatula. When it is cool enough to touch, by hand carefully pull out the brittle to make it thinner. Place the brittle in a kitchen towel and crush with a rolling pin or mallet. Transfer to a bowl and add the oil.

Place the gaufrette cookies in a kitchen towel and crush with a rolling pin or mallet. Add to the brittle in the bowl. In the top of a double boiler, melt the milk chocolate. Add to the bowl. Stir well and transfer the mixture to the plastic-wrap-lined pan. Refrigerate until needed. In the top of a double boiler, melt the dark chocolate. Transfer to a clean bowl. When cool, fold in the cream, add the liqueur, and mix thoroughly. Spread over the milk chocolate mixture in the pan and refrigerate for at least 2 hours, or preferably overnight. Remove the chocolate from the pan and transfer to a flat work surface.

Remove and discard the plastic wrap. Cut the chocolate into oblong bars or the desired shapes. Dust with cocoa powder before serving.

To prepare the anglaise, in a bowl, whisk together the egg yolks and the sugar. In a saucepan, bring the milk and vanilla bean and seeds to a boil. Stir $1/2$ cup of the hot milk into the egg mixture, then pour the milk and egg mixture back into the saucepan. Reduce the heat to medium. Cook, stirring constantly, until the mixture thickens and coats the back of a wooden spoon; do not overcook. Strain into a stainless steel bowl and place in an ice bath to cool. When cool, stir once more and refrigerate until needed.

To prepare the chocolate sauce, place the chocolate in a small, deep bowl. In a saucepan, bring the cream to a boil. Pour over the chocolate and stir until smooth. Keep at room temperature until ready to use; heat over a water bath if the sauce becomes too thick and cold.

To serve, spoon a pool of anglaise on individual plates. Swirl in the chocolate sauce. Artistically arrange pieces of the crunch bar in a pile next to the anglaise. Garnish with the berries.

YIELD: 6 TO 8 SERVINGS

Hawaiian Vintage Chocolate Crunch Bars, pictured with a pulled sugar garnish, as we serve it at the restaurant.

Tropical Ice Cream Trio

Because of the climate, frozen desserts are ever popular in Hawaii. At Alan Wong's, we usually offer a selection of housemade ice creams to satisfy the demand for a plain, simple, yet deliciously flavored dessert. The ice creams in this recipe feature the exotically tropical fruit flavors typical of the islands. Guava and mango purée is available frozen or bottled in Asian markets. Serve the cookies plain, or sprinkle the tuile batter with chopped nuts, shredded coconut, or grated chocolate before baking.

Lychee trees were introduced to Hawaii from their native China in the 1870s, shortly after large numbers of Chinese immigrants arrived to work in the plantations. Guavas, which are native to the tropics of South America, were first planted in the islands around 1825. Today, large numbers are grown commercially, and they also grow wild, especially in parts of Kauai.

Guava Ice Cream (this page)
Lychee-Ginger Ice Cream (next page)
Mango–Lime Ice Cream (next page)
12 Tuile Cookies (next page)

Spoon a scoop of each ice cream on individual plates. Accompany each scoop with a cookie.

YIELD: 4 SERVINGS

GUAVA ICE CREAM

4 large egg yolks
1/2 cup sugar
Pinch of salt
1 3/4 cups heavy cream
3/4 cup guava purée
1/4 cup corn syrup
1 1/2 tablespoons freshly squeezed lemon juice

To prepare the Guava Ice Cream, in a bowl, combine the egg yolks, sugar, and salt. Using a wire whisk, mix until thick, creamy, and light in color. In a nonreactive saucepan, bring the cream, guava purée, corn syrup, and lemon juice to a boil. Stir 1/2 cup of this mixture into the egg mixture, then pour the cream and egg mixture back into the saucepan. Reduce the heat to medium. Cook, stirring constantly, until the mixture thickens and coats the back of a wooden spoon; do not overcook. Strain into a stainless steel bowl and cool over ice water. Transfer to an ice cream machine and freeze according to the manufacturer's directions.

YIELD: 4 SERVINGS

LYCHEE-GINGER ICE CREAM

4 large egg yolks

$^1/_2$ cup sugar

Pinch of salt

12 ounces fresh lychees, peeled and seeded, or 20 ounces canned lychees in syrup, drained

2 ounces ginger, chopped

$1^3/_4$ cups heavy cream

$^1/_4$ cup corn syrup

To prepare the Lychee-Ginger Ice Cream, in a bowl, combine the egg yolks, sugar, and salt. Using a wire whisk, mix until thick, creamy, and light in color. Place half the lychees in a blender and add the ginger. Purée until smooth. Transfer to a nonreactive saucepan, add the cream and corn syrup, and bring to a boil. Reduce the heat and simmer for 5 minutes to let the flavors infuse. Strain into a clean saucepan and reheat. Stir $^1/_2$ cup of this mixture into the egg mixture, then pour the cream and egg mixture back into the saucepan. Reduce the heat to medium. Cook, stirring constantly, until the mixture thickens and coats the back of a wooden spoon; do not overcook. Strain into a stainless steel bowl and cool over ice water. Transfer to an ice cream machine and freeze according to the manufacturer's directions. Dice the remaining lychees, fold into the ice cream, and refreeze until needed.

YIELD: 4 SERVINGS

MANGO-LIME ICE CREAM

4 large egg yolks

$^1/_2$ cup sugar

Pinch of salt

$1^3/_4$ cups heavy cream

$^1/_2$ cup mango purée

$^1/_4$ cup corn syrup

Juice of 1 lime

To prepare the Mango-Lime Ice Cream, in a bowl, combine the egg yolks, sugar, and salt. Using a wire whisk, mix until thick, creamy, and light in color. In a nonreactive saucepan, bring the cream, mango purée, corn syrup, and lime juice to a boil. Stir $^1/_2$ cup of this mixture into the egg mixture, then pour the cream and egg mixture back into the saucepan. Reduce the heat to medium. Cook, stirring constantly, until the mixture thickens and coats the back of a wooden spoon; do not overcook. Strain into a stainless steel bowl and cool over ice water. Transfer to an ice cream machine and freeze according to the manufacturer's directions.

YIELD: 4 SERVINGS

TUILE COOKIES

5 tablespoons butter

$^1/_2$ cup sugar

5 tablespoons flour

3 egg whites

1 teaspoon vanilla extract

To prepare the cookies, preheat the oven to 350°. Grease a baking sheet. In the bowl of an electric mixer fitted with a beater attachment, cream the butter and sugar together until well blended. Add the flour and continue to mix until smooth. Add the egg whites, one at a time, scraping down the sides of the bowl and mixing until smooth after each addition. Mix in the vanilla. Half-fill a parchment paper pastry bag with the batter and carefully cut off the tip of the bag. Onto the baking sheet, pipe about 24 strips of batter 6 inches long, $^1/_4$ inch wide, and 2 inches apart. Bake for 12 minutes, or until golden brown. Using a spatula, remove the cookie strips while they are still warm and wrap them in a spiral around the handle of wooden spoons. Alternatively, leave the cookies flat. Store extra cookies in an airtight container and serve with future ice cream desserts.

YIELD: 24 COOKIES

The Coconut

Abigail Langlas came up with this idea for a dessert, simply called "The Coconut." At first, many guests left the outer "shell" uneaten because it looks so lifelike. We have taken to mentioning that it is not really a coconut, but made of premium Hawaiian Vintage chocolate (see page 150), which solved the problem! The haupia sorbet is best used as soon as it has finished freezing, as it's easier to work with then. For those who are allergic to latex, instead of using a balloon as a mold, use a large orange covered in plastic wrap.

HAUPIA SORBET

3 cups extra-rich (25 percent) coconut milk or canned unsweetened coconut milk

1 1/2 cups water (if using extra-rich coconut milk) or canned unsweetened coconut milk

3 cups Simple Syrup (page 183)

COCONUT SHELLS

6 (4-inch) rubber balloons

1 pound Hawaiian Vintage bittersweet chocolate

1 1/4 cups coconut flakes, toasted

LILIKOI SAUCE

1/4 cup passion fruit purée with seeds

2 1/2 tablespoons sugar

1/2 cup water

1/2 tablespoon cornstarch

MIXED TROPICAL FRUITS

1 banana, sliced

1/2 mango or papaya, diced

1/4 pineapple, diced

1/2 cup diced fresh or canned lychees

2 starfruit, sliced

1/4 cup melted Hawaiian Vintage bittersweet chocolate

6 mint sprigs, for garnish

To prepare the sorbet, in a bowl, thoroughly combine the coconut milk, water, and syrup. Transfer to an ice cream machine and freeze according to the manufacturer's directions.

To prepare the coconut shells, line a baking sheet with parchment or waxed paper. Inflate the balloons to a diameter of about 4 inches and tightly secure the ends. In the top of a double boiler, melt two thirds of the chocolate to 120° on a candy thermometer. Add the remaining chocolate and mix with a spatula until completely melted. Dip the rounded (nonstem) half of each balloon in the chocolate, rotating to cover thoroughly, and sprinkle with the toasted coconut flakes. Set the half-covered balloons at an angle on the prepared baking sheet until the chocolate sets and is hard. Pop the balloons; remove and discard all the rubber pieces. Freeze the shells until you are ready to fill them.

Using a tablespoon, carefully spoon the sorbet into the chocolate shells and gently pack down. Carefully scoop out the center of the sorbet to resemble the coconut meat and smooth out the edges using a spatula or knife. Return to the freezer.

To prepare the sauce, in a saucepan, bring the passion fruit, sugar, and all but 1 tablespoon of the water to a boil. In a cup, mix the cornstarch with the remaining water until dissolved and add to the pan. Cook until the sauce is slightly thickened and coats the back of a wooden spoon. Chill.

To prepare Mixed Topical Fruits, in a bowl, combine the banana, mango or papaya, pineapple, lychees, and star fruit. Refrigerate until needed.

To serve, spoon the melted chocolate onto the center of individual plates and, while still warm, top with the coconuts; as the chocolate hardens, it will secure the coconuts in place. Divide the mixed fruit among the plates, in and around the coconut. Drizzle with the sauce. Garnish with the mint sprigs.

YIELD: 6 SERVINGS

"To the American or European, nibbling a coconut candy bar or savoring a cake with shredded coconut in its frosting or eating a slice of coconut custard pie, the coconut may seem no more than an airy trifle, agreeably exotic but easily dispensable; yet for one-third of the population of this planet, the coconut is regarded as one of the most important foods in the world." —Waverly Root, *Food*

Waimea Strawberry Tart
with Hawaiian Vintage White Chocolate Ice Cream and Macadamia Nut Shortbread

This dessert specifically showcases the luscious Waimea strawberries, although you can use other kinds of quality fresh strawberries. Without a doubt, this dessert is best made when strawberries are in peak season, and preferably with vine-ripened berries.

HAWAIIAN VINTAGE WHITE CHOCOLATE ICE CREAM

4 egg yolks

6 tablespoons sugar

Pinch of salt

1 cup plus 2 tablespoons heavy cream

1 cup plus 2 tablespoons milk

8 ounces (1^1/$_4$ cups) Hawaiian Vintage white chocolate drops or coins

WHITE CHOCOLATE PASTRY CREAM

1 cup milk

^{1}/$_4$ cup sugar

2 tablespoons butter

^{1}/$_2$ vanilla bean, halved lengthwise and seeds scraped

2 egg yolks

1^1/$_2$ tablespoons cornstarch

2 tablespoons melted Hawaiian Vintage white chocolate

MACADAMIA NUT SHORTBREAD

^{1}/$_2$ cup butter, at room temperature

^{1}/$_4$ cup sugar

Pinch of salt

1^1/$_3$ cups flour

^{1}/$_2$ cup chopped macadamia nuts

2 tablespoons Hawaiian Vintage chocolate drops or coins

STRAWBERRY COULIS

1 cup strawberries

1 teaspoon sugar

CRÈME ANGLAISE

2 extra-large egg yolks

^{1}/$_4$ cup sugar

^{2}/$_3$ cup milk

^{1}/$_2$ vanilla bean, halved lengthwise and seeds scraped

4 cups Waimea strawberries, halved

To prepare the ice cream, in a bowl, combine the egg yolks, sugar, and salt. Using a wire whisk, mix until thick, creamy, and light in color. In a saucepan over medium heat, bring the cream and milk to a boil. Stir ^{1}/$_2$ cup of the cream mixture into the egg mixture, then pour the cream and egg mixture back into the saucepan. Add the chocolate, stirring until the chocolate has melted and is thoroughly incorporated. Cook, stirring constantly, until the mixture thickens and coats the back of a wooden spoon; do not overcook. Strain into a stainless steel bowl and cool over ice water. Transfer to an ice cream machine and freeze according to the manufacturer's directions.

Hawaiian Vintage is the only chocolate grown in the United States, and it is a product of the highest quality. The cacao beans are grown in Kona and Keaau on the Big Island, aged for a year, and processed in California. The chocolate is sold according to its year of vintage, hence the name of the company. Like wine, each vintage has subtle nuances and differences of flavor such as a hint of berry or nuts, and some vintages are a little more acidic than others. It is another local food product of which Hawaii is justifiably proud.

To prepare the pastry cream, in a small saucepan, bring all but 2 tablespoons of the milk, the sugar, butter, and vanilla bean and seeds to a boil. Meanwhile, in a bowl, whisk together the egg yolks, cornstarch, and the remaining 2 tablespoons of milk. Whisk the egg mixture into the saucepan. Return to a boil and immediately remove from the heat. Stir in the melted chocolate. Transfer to a bowl, cover immediately with plastic wrap to prevent a crust from forming, and refrigerate until needed.

To prepare the shortbread, preheat the oven to 350°. In a mixer fitted with a paddle attachment, mix the butter, sugar, and salt on low speed until smooth. Add the flour and thoroughly incorporate. Add the nuts and chocolate and combine but do not overmix. Turn the dough out onto a lightly floured surface and roll out to a thickness of $^1/_4$ inch. Using a cookie cutter, cut out rounds 4 inches in diameter. Transfer to a baking sheet. Bake for about 12 minutes, or until the edges are golden brown. Let cool.

To prepare the coulis, in a blender combine the strawberries and sugar. Purée until smooth. Refrigerate until needed.

To prepare the anglaise, in a bowl, using a wire whisk, beat the egg yolks and sugar. In a heavy-bottomed saucepan, bring the milk and vanilla bean and seeds to a boil. Stir half of the hot milk mixture into the eggs, then pour the milk and egg mixture back into the saucepan. Reduce the heat to medium and stir constantly with a wooden spoon until the mixture thickens enough to coat the back of the spoon. Strain into a stainless steel bowl and place in an ice bath to cool; keep stirring for 2 to 3 minutes, or until it stops steaming. Refrigerate until needed.

To serve, place the pastry cream in a pastry bag fitted with a plain round $^3/_8$-inch tube. Pipe the cream in a circular pattern over each shortbread crust. Arrange the strawberry halves in a circular pattern, with the bases embedded in the cream and the cut sides facing outwards. Place each tart in the center of an individual plate. Spoon a scoop of ice cream in the center of each tart on top of the berries. Pour the anglaise around each tart and drizzle the coulis in a back-and-forth motion over the tart.

YIELD: 4 SERVINGS

Some of the choicest strawberries I have ever tasted came from Waimea on the Big Island. The moist, cool climate at the elevation of 2,500 feet obviously suits the Japanese variety of berries to perfection, as their intense color and flavor suggest. Waimea strawberries are in season from November until early summer, and we are fortunate to have such an extended growing season.

Tropical Sorbet Martinis

This is a cool way to enjoy frozen tropical cocktails. Since these sorbets contain alcohol, the sorbets will be softer and separate faster than regular fruit sorbets, and you may need to extend the freezing time. You will want to keep these sorbets out of the reach of passing children and pets! Except for the Blue Hawaii, you can make the sorbets without alcohol so that kids can enjoy them, and then serve a little rum in the bottom of each adult's glass before adding the sorbets.

MAI TAI SORBET

3/4 cup **Simple Syrup (page 183)**

1 1/2 cups **pineapple juice**

1/4 cup **orgeat syrup**

1 tablespoon **freshly squeezed lemon juice**

1 teaspoon **orange curaçao**

1 tablespoon **dark rum**

1 tablespoon **amber rum**

CHI CHI SORBET

2 cups **pineapple juice**

1 cup **coconut syrup**

1/2 tablespoon **freshly squeezed lemon juice**

1 tablespoon **coconut-flavored Malibu rum**

BLUE HAWAII SORBET

1/2 cup **Simple Syrup (page 183)**

2 1/2 cups **pineapple juice**

1 tablespoon **freshly squeezed lemon juice**

1/2 cup **blue curaçao**

PLANTER'S PUNCH SORBET

3/4 cup **pineapple juice**

3/4 cup **passion fruit juice**

3/4 cup **freshly squeezed orange juice**

1 teaspoon **Angostura bitters**

1/2 cup **grenadine**

1 teaspoon **orange curaçao**

1 teaspoon **dark rum**

6 sprigs **mint, for garnish**

Mixed Tropical Fruits (page 148), for garnish (optional)

To prepare each sorbet, in bowls, thoroughly combine the ingredients. Transfer each batch to an ice cream machine and freeze according to the manufacturer's directions.

To serve, spoon a large scoop of each sorbet into large martini glasses. Garnish with a mint sprig, mixed fruits, and a paper umbrella pick, if desired.

YIELD: 6 SERVINGS

Okinawan Sweet Potato Cheesecake
with Azuki Bean Relish and Haupia Sauce

This is my Pacific version of the classic Southern sweet potato pie, but the flavors and colors are quite unlike any sweet potato dessert you've ever tried! Okinawan sweet potatoes, which are grown in Hawaii, are purple, with a uniquely sweet flavor and creamy texture that is particularly enhanced by the coconut milk. I thought of using Okinawan sweet potatoes in a dessert after experimenting with pumpkin cheesecake one fall, and the consistency is very similar. The azuki relish, based on the Japanese red beans, continues the Asian theme, while the haupia gives the whole dish a distinctively Hawaiian touch.

CRUST

2 tablespoons butter, melted

$1/2$ cup graham cracker crumbs

$1/4$ cup sugar

CHEESECAKE

$3/4$ cup peeled and cubed Okinawan sweet potato or regular sweet potato

$1/4$ cup plus 2 tablespoons canned unsweetened coconut milk

$1/8$ teaspoon minced ginger

$1/2$ tablespoon sugar

12 ounces cream cheese

$3/4$ cup sugar

2 eggs plus 1 egg yolk

1 tablespoon dark rum

HAUPIA AND HAUPIA SAUCE

$3/4$ cup canned unsweetened coconut milk

$1/4$ cup sugar

$2 1/2$ tablespoons arrowroot

$1/2$ cup water

AZUKI BEAN RELISH

1 cup dried azuki beans, soaked in water overnight

5 cups water

$1/2$ cup sugar

SWEET POTATO CHIPS

Vegetable oil for deep-frying

1 small Okinawan sweet potato or regular sweet potato, cut into 12 slices

$1/4$ cup sugar

18 sections Ka'u or navel orange, for garnish

6 mint sprigs, for garnish

To prepare the crust, line the bottom and sides of a 6-inch cake pan with parchment paper. In a bowl, combine the butter, cracker crumbs, and sugar. Press into the bottom of the cake pan. Set aside.

Preheat the oven to 350°.

To prepare the cheesecake, place the sweet potato in a steamer or vegetable basket set in a saucepan of lightly boiling water. Cover and steam for about 15 minutes, or until tender. Meanwhile, in a small saucepan, bring the $1/4$ cup of coconut milk, ginger, and sugar to a boil. Reduce the heat to low and simmer for 10 minutes to let the flavors develop. Reserve 4 tablespoons of the sweet potatoes for the azuki relish. In a bowl, combine the remaining potatoes and 3 tablespoons of the coconut milk mixture. Mash until the potatoes are smooth.

In a mixer fitted with a paddle attachment on low speed, cream the cheese for about 5 minutes, or until smooth. Add the hot sweet potato mixture and sugar and continue beating on low speed, stopping the mixer occasionally to scrape down the sides of the bowl with a rubber spatula. Add the eggs and yolk, one at a time, letting the mixture incorporate before each new addition. Mix in the rum and 2 tablespoons of coconut milk. Pour the batter over the crust in the cake pan. Place the cake in a larger baking pan and fill the larger pan with water until the liquid comes two thirds of the way up the sides of the cake pan. If using a springform pan, place the water pan on the bottom oven rack below the cheesecake. Bake for 1 hour. Let cool.

Haupia is the traditional Hawaiian dessert invariably served at luaus. Unfortunately, most tourists who attend commercial luaus taste a mass-produced, stodgy version made with cornstarch. The genuine article, which has a delightfully delicate flavor, contains *pia*, powdered Polynesian arrowroot. Alternatively, use a good-quality arrowroot from a natural foods store. In ancient times, haupia was wrapped in ti leaves and steamed in the *imu*.

To prepare the haupia and haupia sauce, line a small baking pan measuring 4 or 6 inches square with plastic wrap. In a small saucepan, bring the coconut milk and sugar to a boil. Remove from the heat. In a bowl, dissolve the arrowroot in $1/4$ cup of the water and stir into the pan. Return the mixture to a boil and remove from the heat once more. Pour half of the haupia mixture into the prepared pan. Cover, cool, and set in the refrigerator. In a saucepan, bring the remaining $1/4$ cup of water to a boil. Add the remaining haupia mixture and return to a boil. Remove from the heat and let cool.

To prepare the relish, drain and rinse the beans. In a saucepan, bring the beans and water to a boil. Boil for 30 minutes, or until just tender. Add the sugar and boil for 15 minutes. Drain, place in a bowl, and let cool. Dice the reserved 4 tablespoons of the sweet potato and set aside. Remove the haupia from the refrigerator when it has set, dice, and set aside.

To prepare the sweet potato chips, in a deep fryer or large, heavy saucepan over high heat, heat about 3 inches of vegetable oil to 350°. Deep-fry the potato slices until crisp. Remove and drain on paper towels. Place the sugar on a plate and dredge the potato slices in the sugar.

To serve, divide the haupia sauce among individual plates. With a knife dipped in hot water, cut the cheesecake into 12 thin slices, wiping the knife after each cut and dipping again in hot water. Arrange 2 slices on the sauce on each plate; place one piece at an angle near the center of the plate and the other on its end so the point is in the air and the crust end is lying on the plate. Fan 3 orange segments to one side of the cake and place 2 tablespoons of the relish between the slices of cheesecake. Top the relish with the diced sweet potato and haupia. Garnish with a mint sprig. Top each slice of cake with a sweet potato chip.

YIELD: 6 SERVINGS

Baked Hawaii

This sublime dessert is our unique take on the classic Baked Alaska, containing the same essential ingredients—sponge cake, ice cream or sorbet, and meringue—but translated into a uniquely Hawaiian style. There is no getting around the fact that this is a complex recipe, but we are constantly asked for it and I wanted to include it for our more ambitious readers. There are three flavors of sorbet used here, so if you own one ice cream machine, you will need to make one sorbet at a time and transfer it to a storage container before making the others. You will need a kitchen propane blowtorch to brown the meringue. These hand-held torches, available at specialty kitchen stores, are useful for many other purposes, such as roasting chiles and browning brûlées. To simplify the recipe a little, omit the Pineapple Truffles, Guava Anglaise, and white chocolate edging, leaving a dessert that is still most impressive.

PINEAPPLE SORBET

1 cup Simple Syrup (page 183)

3 cups pineapple juice

2 teaspoons freshly squeezed
  lemon juice

GUAVA SORBET

1 1/4 cups Simple Syrup (page 183)

1 1/4 cups pink guava purée

1 1/4 cups water

2 teaspoons freshly squeezed
  lime juice

LILIKOI SORBET

1 1/2 cups Simple Syrup (page 183)

1 cup passion fruit purée

2 cups water

CHOCOLATE
PINEAPPLE LEAVES

20 pineapple leaves

4 ounces Hawaiian Vintage
  white chocolate

4 or 5 drops green food coloring

WHITE CHOCOLATE LATTICE

5 ounces Hawaiian Vintage
  white chocolate

PINEAPPLE TRUFFLES

1 cup pineapple juice

1 tablespoon butter

2 tablespoons heavy cream

1 egg yolk, beaten

6 ounces Hawaiian Vintage white
  chocolate

1 teaspoon freshly squeezed
  lemon juice

1 cup toasted coconut flakes

GUAVA ANGLAISE

2 egg yolks

3 tablespoons sugar

6 tablespoons milk

2 tablespoons pink guava purée

Juice of 1/2 a lemon

1 small round sponge cake,
  cut to 1/4 inch thick

MERINGUE

1 1/2 cups sugar

3/4 cup egg whites (from about
  6 eggs)

1 teaspoon freshly squeezed
  lemon juice

4 ounces white chocolate coating

1/2 pineapple, diced, for garnish

To prepare the Pineapple Sorbet, in a bowl, combine the Simple Syrup, pineapple juice, and lemon juice. Transfer to an ice cream machine and freeze according to the manufacturer's directions.

To prepare the Guava Sorbet, in a bowl combine the Simple Syrup, the guava purée, water, and lime juice. Transfer to an ice cream machine and freeze according to the manufacturer's directions.

To prepare the Lilikoi Sorbet, in a bowl, combine the Simple Syrup, the passion fruit purée, and water. Transfer to an ice cream machine and freeze according to the manufacturer's directions.

To make the Chocolate Pineapple Leaves, wash and dry the pineapple leaves. In the top of a double boiler, gently melt the white chocolate. Add the green coloring. Using a 1/2-inch pastry brush, paint 2 coats of chocolate on the underside of the leaves, letting the chocolate harden after each coat. Refrigerate the leaves to harden. When hard, carefully peel off the chocolate from each leaf; discard the

(continued)

The town of Wahiawa in central Oahu, where I grew up, is a community that has been based on the pineapple ever since the late 1800s, when the first pineapple plantations were established. As a youngster, like many of my friends, I lived and worked in the pineapple fields; one summer, I remember earning $1.60 an hour and losing 60 pounds. The fruit is the international symbol of hospitality, which, in addition to its personal significance for me, is why I chose it as the logo for Alan Wong's restaurant.

The pineapple, the fruit of a perennial herb native to Central and South America, was introduced to Hawaii in 1813 by the Spanish horticulturist Don Marin. By the 1940s, the Dole and Del Monte companies were growing 80 percent of the world's pineapples in Hawaii. Lanai became known as "The Pineapple Island" because the largest single pineapple plantation in the world dominated the landscape. Thousands of acres around Wahiawa and large parts of Maui were also devoted to the industry, and my hometown was a major cannery center. Over recent years, however, much of the industry has left Hawaii for Southeast Asia, where the costs of land and labor are lower. The pineapple is such an important part of Hawaii's history that it would truly be tragic if the remaining plantations were ever to close.

(continued)

pineapple leaves and refrigerate the chocolate leaves until ready to serve.

To prepare the chocolate lattice, in the top of a double boiler, gently melt the white chocolate. Using a paper pastry bag with a cut tip, pipe the chocolate onto a cool surface in a lattice pattern. Let cool.

To prepare the truffles, in a nonreactive saucepan, bring the pineapple juice to a boil. Simmer until reduced to 2 tablespoons and the concentrate has a jamlike consistency. Let cool slightly. Add the butter and cream to the pan and bring to a boil. Add the egg yolk and cook for 4 to 5 minutes, or until the mixture thickens. Stir in the white chocolate and lemon juice and heat, stirring, until the chocolate melts. Remove from the heat, pour the mixture into a container, and refrigerate until needed. Just before serving, place the coconut on a plate. Scoop out approximately 2 teaspoons of the chilled truffle mixture, form into a ball, and roll in the coconut. Repeat for the remaining 8 truffles.

To prepare the anglaise, in a bowl, beat the egg yolks and the sugar.

In a nonreactive saucepan, bring the milk, guava, and lemon juice to a boil. Stir half of this mixture into the egg mixture. Pour the egg and milk mixture back into the saucepan. Reduce the heat to medium. Cook, stirring constantly, until the mixture thickens and coats the back of a wooden spoon; do not overcook. Strain into a stainless steel bowl and cool over ice water.

Place a 4-inch square of parchment paper on a flat plate. Use a 2-inch-diameter by 1 1/2-inch-high cylindrical stainless steel mold or cookie cutter to cut a circle of the sponge cake. Fit the cake into the bottom of the mold to form the base of the dessert. Scoop approximately 3 tablespoons of each sorbet and layer inside the mold on top of the cake. Work quickly to form a mound rising above the rim of the mold. Freeze to reset. Repeat for the remaining 3 servings.

To prepare the meringue, in the top of a double boiler, combine the sugar, egg whites, and lemon juice. Heat until the sugar dissolves. Remove from the heat. Using an electric mixer at high speed, beat until thick. Let cool.

Remove the molds from the cake and sorbet. Spoon the meringue into a pastry bag fitted with a round 3/8-inch tube and pipe over the molded sorbets in spiky peaks to resemble the skin of a pineapple. Return to the freezer.

To assemble the dessert, in the top of a double boiler, melt the white chocolate coating. Using a paper pastry bag with a cut tip, pipe the chocolate into 3 leaf outline shapes pointing outward from the center of individual plates. Fill each leaf outline with Guava Anglaise. Remove the sorbet pineapples from the freezer, remove the parchment paper base, and place in the center of the 3-leaf design. Using a hand-held propane torch, brown the meringue. Arrange the chocolate leaves sticking out from the top of the meringue to resemble pineapple leaves. Place a truffle on each plate between two of the anglaise leaves. Gently cut or break the chocolate lattice into small squares. Stand one square upright in each truffle, for garnish. Sprinkle the diced pineapple between each of the anglaise leaves.

YIELD: 4 SERVINGS

Five Spoonfuls of Brûlée

We serve this assortment of Hawaiian-flavored brûlées in Chinese porcelain soup spoons instead of the traditional ramekins. For locals, especially, these soup spoons typify down-home *saimin* and bowls of noodles, and the last place you would expect to find them is on a dessert plate! Each spoon holds about 2 tablespoons of brûlée. If you use $1/4$-cup ramekins instead, half-fill them. You will need to prepare one brûlée at a time, making this recipe labor-intensive, but they can be prepared ahead of time.

Macadamia Nut Brûlée (this page)

Hawaiian Vintage Chocolate Brûlée (this page)

Ka'u Orange Brûlée (page 161)

Kona Mocha Brûlée (page 161)

Lilikoi Brûlée (page 161)

Zest of $1/2$ orange, finely julienned

$1/4$ cup water

$1/4$ cup plus 5 tablespoons sugar

$1/2$ teaspoon finely diced macadamia nuts

6 curls shaved Hawaiian Vintage chocolate or other good-quality chocolate

6 coffee beans

Pulp of 1 passion fruit

Arrange 1 spoon of each brûlée on individual plates.

In a small saucepan, combine the orange zest, water, and $1/4$ cup of the sugar. Boil for 10 minutes, or until syrupy. Drain the zest. Sprinkle $1/2$ teaspoon of sugar over the brûlée in each spoon. Place the brûlée under the broiler for about 30 seconds, or until the sugar caramelizes.

To serve, top the macadamia brûlée with the nuts, the chocolate brûlée with the shaved chocolate, the orange brûlée with the candied zest, the kona brûlée with the coffee beans, and the lilikoi brûlée with the passion fruit.

YIELD: 6 SERVINGS

MACADAMIA NUT BRÛLÉE

$1/2$ cup heavy cream

3 extra-large egg yolks

2 tablespoons sugar

$1/2$ tablespoon butter

$1/2$ tablespoon macadamia nut liqueur

2 tablespoons ground macadamia nuts

To prepare the Macadamia Nut Brûlée, in a small saucepan, slowly bring $1/2$ cup of the cream, macadamia nut liqueur, and nuts to a boil. Simmer gently for 5 minutes. Meanwhile, place 3 of the egg yolks and 2 tablespoons of the sugar in the top of a double boiler over medium-low heat. Cook, stirring constantly using a wire whisk, for about 10 minutes, or until very thick. Add the boiling cream mixture and $1/2$ tablespoon of the butter, stirring to combine. Remove from the heat. Half-submerge the top of the double boiler in a bowl of ice and stir the mixture for 2 to 3 minutes, or until it stops steaming. Fill 6 Chinese porcelain soup spoons with the mixture and chill.

HAWAIIAN VINTAGE CHOCOLATE BRÛLÉE

$1/2$ cups heavy cream

3 extra-large egg yolks

2 tablespoons sugar

$1/2$ tablespoons butter

$1/4$ cup Hawaiian Vintage chocolate drops or coins, or other good-quality chocolate, chopped

To prepare the chocolate brûlée, in a small saucepan, slowly bring $1/2$ cup of the cream to a boil. Simmer gently for 5 minutes. Meanwhile, place 3 of the egg yolks and 2 tablespoons of the sugar in the top of a double boiler over medium-low heat. Cook, stirring constantly using a wire whisk, for about 10 minutes, or until very thick. Add the boiling cream mixture, $1/2$ tablespoon of the butter, and the chocolate. Cook, stirring, until the chocolate has melted and is thoroughly incorporated. Remove from the heat. Half-submerge the top of the double boiler in a bowl of ice and stir the mixture for 2 to 3 minutes, or until it stops steaming. Fill 6 Chinese porcelain soup spoons with the mixture and chill.

(continued)

(continued)

KA'U ORANGE BRÛLÉE

$1/2$ **cup heavy cream**

3 extra-large egg yolks

2 tablespoons sugar

$1/2$ **tablespoon butter**

Zest of $1/2$ Ka'u or navel orange, grated

To prepare the orange brûlée, in a small saucepan, slowly bring $1/2$ cup of the cream and the orange zest to a boil. Simmer gently for 5 minutes. Meanwhile, place 3 of the egg yolks and 2 tablespoons of the sugar in the top of a double boiler over medium-low heat. Cook, stirring constantly using a wire whisk, for about 10 minutes, or until very thick. Add the boiling cream mixture and $1/2$ tablespoon of the butter, stirring to combine. Remove from the heat. Half-submerge the top of the double boiler in a bowl of ice and stir the mixture for 2 to 3 minutes, or until it stops steaming. Fill 6 Chinese porcelain soup spoons with the mixture and chill.

KONA MOCHA BRÛLÉE

$1/2$ **cup heavy cream**

3 extra-large egg yolks

2 tablespoons sugar

$1/2$ **tablespoon butter**

$1/2$ **tablespoon ground Kona espresso beans**

2 tablespoons Hawaiian Vintage chocolate drops or coins

To prepare the Kona Mocha Brûlée, in a small saucepan, slowly bring $1/2$ cup of the cream and ground espresso beans to a boil. Simmer gently for 5 minutes. Meanwhile, place 3 of the egg yolks and 2 tablespoons of the sugar in the top of a double boiler over medium-low heat. Cook, stirring constantly using a wire whisk, for about 10 minutes, or until very thick. Add the boiling cream mixture, $1/2$ tablespoon of the butter, and the chocolate, stirring until the chocolate has melted and is thoroughly incorporated. Remove from the heat. Half-submerge the top of the double boiler in a bowl of ice and stir the mixture for 2 to 3 minutes, or until it stops steaming. Fill 6 Chinese porcelain soup spoons with the mixture and chill.

LILIKOI BRÛLÉE

$1/2$ **cup heavy cream**

3 extra-large egg yolks

2 tablespoons sugar

$1/2$ **tablespoon butter**

2 tablespoons passion fruit pulp and seeds (from 2 passion fruits) or passion fruit concentrate

To prepare the Lilikoi Brûlée, in a small saucepan, slowly bring the remaining $1/2$ cup of the cream and passion fruit to a boil. Simmer gently for 5 minutes. Meanwhile, place the remaining 3 egg yolks and remaining 2 tablespoons of the sugar in the top of a double boiler over medium-low heat. Cook, stirring constantly using a wire whisk, for about 10 minutes, or until very thick. Add the boiling cream mixture and remaining $1/2$ tablespoon of butter, stirring to combine. Remove from the heat. Half-submerge the top of the double boiler in a bowl of ice and stir the mixture for 2 to 3 minutes, or until it stops steaming. Fill 6 Chinese porcelain soup spoons with the mixture and chill.

Drinks

Drinks

At Alan Wong's, we take pride in our cocktail menu. My cocktail philosophy is that they should be fun and incorporate the wealth of luscious tropical fruits that grow in abundance on the Hawaiian Islands. Cocktails that satisfy these important criteria make a statement in their own right and set up the food that follows. This is as true when entertaining in your home as it is in any restaurant.

Sean Nakamura, the trusty bartender at Alan Wong's, devised most of the cocktail recipes that follow. Sean, who grew up on the Big Island and qualified as a civil engineer at the University of Hawaii, has done an excellent job of very civilly engineering a drinks menu that matches our fine wines and innovative food. I take the credit for challenging Sean to use his creativity and imagination—as well as local produce—and he has not disappointed. Although Sean will serve our guests a classic Mai Tai, Blue Hawaiian, or Singapore Sling, the cocktails in this chapter are those that we proudly highlight on our menu, and that are the most popular with our guests.

Kolohe Hawaiian

Kolohe is a Hawaiian word meaning nutty, crazy, or rascal, which is the way you will feel if you try too many of these cocktails. Perhaps it's the macadamia nut liqueur and chopped macadamias that give this drink that rascally feeling.

2 tablespoons Malibu
    coconut-flavored rum

2 tablespoons macadamia nut liqueur
    or Frangelico

1 scoop vanilla ice cream

1/4 cup half-and-half

1 cup ice

2 tablespoons Hawaiian Vintage
    chocolate syrup or regular
    chocolate syrup

1 tablespoon whipped cream

1/2 teaspoon chopped macadamia nuts

In a blender, combine the rum, macadamia nut liqueur, ice cream, half-and-half, and ice and purée until thick and smooth. Pour the chocolate syrup in the bottom of a large wine glass and swirl to coat the bottom one-third of the glass. Add the blended mixture. Top with whipped cream and sprinkle with the nuts.

YIELD: I COCKTAIL

Tangerine Tickle

This drink is a seasonal item at Alan Wong's because to do it justice, it must be made with fresh tangerine juice. We use the wintertime abundance of Big Island tangerines, but you can also use the juice of fresh mandarins or other oranges. The citrus tones of the rum, Triple Sec, sweet-and-sour mix, and Grand Marnier give the predominant flavor of the tangerine juice an intriguing complexity.

Ice

2 1/2 tablespoons Bacardi Limón

1 tablespoon Triple Sec

1/2 cup freshly squeezed tangerine
    juice

1 tablespoon sweet-and-sour mix

2 tablespoons 7-Up

1/2 tablespoon Grand Marnier

Place the ice in a zombie glass. Add the Limón, Triple Sec, tangerine juice, sweet-and-sour mix, and 7-Up and stir gently. Carefully float the Grand Marnier on top.

YIELD: I COCKTAIL

Bully's Pineapple Martini

By painstaking research and numerous sips of this cocktail, I discovered that 3 days was the optimum time for letting the pineapple macerate in the vodka—it was fun doing the testing two or three times a day to arrive at this conclusion. The original recipe called for sweet, low-acid Sugarloaf white pineapples, but lately, we've taken to using the new local yellow pineapples for their sweetness, hints of coconut flavor, and attractive color. These martinis are so sweet, yet so strong, that we don't recommend trying more than one of them at a time.

1 liter triple-distilled premium vodka

2 large ripe pineapples, peeled, cored, and cut into small cubes

In a large glass jar, combine the vodka and pineapple and macerate in the refrigerator for 3 days. If the pineapple is less sweet and the mixture still has an alcohol bite to it, add more pineapple and refrigerate for 2 or 3 more days. Strain, reserving 12 to 15 of the pineapple cubes. Pour 1/4 cup of the mixture into each martini glass. Add a reserved pineapple cube.

YIELD: 12 TO 15 COCKTAILS

Bully is an island nickname. "Eh bully," locals say, kind of like "Hey, dude." I first picked up the expression when I was living on Kauai and couldn't remember someone's name. I used it so much, my friends gave me the nickname and it's stuck ever since.

Polynesian Paralysis

As the name suggests, this is another cocktail with a recommended limit of one per guest. First I came up with this name, which refers to the sleepy feeling you get after eating too much, and then I asked our bartender, Sean, to create a tall drink in a hurricane glass. He devised this wonderful layered cocktail. It's meant to be drunk with a straw from the bottom of the glass without stirring or mixing the layers. The coconut-flavored Malibu rum is a great asset to have on hand for use in many tropical drinks. Passion fruit and guava juice are available as frozen concentrate.

Ice

1¹/₂ tablespoons Malibu coconut-flavored rum

¹/₄ cup unsweetened pineapple juice

1¹/₂ tablespoons Captain Morgan's spiced rum

¹/₄ cup passion fruit juice

1¹/₂ tablespoons Bacardi light rum

¹/₄ cup guava juice

1¹/₂ tablespoons Myers's dark rum

1 maraschino cherry

1 mint sprig

1 pineapple wedge, for garnish

Place the ice in a large hurricane glass. Pour in the coconut-flavored rum and pineapple juice. Carefully and slowly pour in the spiced rum and passion fruit juice to create a second layer. Pour in the light rum and guava juice for a third layer. Finally, float the dark rum on top. Add the cherry and mint sprig. Garnish the glass with the pineapple wedge. Serve with a straw.

YIELD: I COCKTAIL

Mango Melange à Trois

The triple flavor combination of passion fruit, coconut, and mango in this smooth tropical cocktail is truly luscious. At the restaurant, we originally made this drink only during the summer mango season when the aromatic, juicy island Hayden mangoes are at their peak. Our regular guests loved it so much they asked for it year round. When mangoes are out of season, substitute mango purée. If Alizé is unavailable, use Grand Marnier.

3 tablespoons Alizé passion fruit cognac

$1/4$ cup passion fruit juice

1 tablespoon coconut syrup or Coco Lopez

$1/3$ fresh mango, peeled, pitted, and coarsely chopped

1 cup ice

In a blender, combine the cognac, passion fruit juice, coconut syrup or Coco Lopez, mango, and ice and purée until smooth. To serve, pour into a large wine glass.

YIELD: I COCKTAIL

The Erup-Sean

Sean originally devised this cocktail for Valentine's Day. He called it The Passionate Embrace and served it in a large hurricane glass with two straws for romantics to share. Its striking marbled cream and carmine color is perfect for such a celebration. When guests asked for it long after Valentine's Day, we made a play on words and named it for its creator. When strawberries are out of season, use $1/4$ cup strawberry purée.

Ice

4 strawberries

2 drops grenadine syrup

6 tablespoons passion fruit juice

2 tablespoons diced ripe sweet apple banana or regular banana

2 tablespoons Bols banana liqueur

$1^1/2$ tablespoons light rum

1 mint sprig, for garnish

Place the ice in a tall pilsner glass. Reserving 1 strawberry for garnish, stem the 3 remaining strawberries. Place in a blender and purée until smooth. Pour over the ice. Add the grenadine. In the blender, combine the passion fruit juice, banana, banana liqueur, and rum and purée until smooth. Pour over the strawberries to create a marbled effect. Split the pointed end of the remaining strawberry with a knife and place on the edge of the glass. Garnish with the mint sprig.

YIELD: I COCKTAIL

Tai Chee

Here's a cocktail named with a play on the words *Tai Chi*, the ancient Chinese art form of body movements to control and move body energy, and *chee* from lychee. Be sure to use fresh lychees when they are in season during June and July. Their delicate, rich flavor and aromatic juiciness are perfectly balanced by the acidity of the lemon juice and citrus-flavored vodka in this truly exotic drink.

4 fresh lychees, pitted, or 4 canned lychees with 1/2 tablespoon syrup

1 tablespoon freshly squeezed lemon juice

2 1/2 tablespoons citrus-flavored vodka

1 cup ice

In a blender, combine the lychees, lemon juice, vodka, and ice and purée until thick and smooth. To serve, pour into a tall pilsner glass.

YIELD: I COCKTAIL

Hemo Presha

Hawaii is a place of innumerable languages and dialects. The pidgin English spoken by the locals has long been a common language denominator among the different ethnic groups, and the name of this cocktail draws on this tradition. Each Hawaiian island has a subtle—and sometimes not so subtle—difference in the pidgin English, so you can usually tell where someone is from this way. *Hemo* is a pidgin word used on Kauai meaning "to remove." It's used in all kinds of contexts: you hemo water when you perspire, you hemo skin if you scrape yourself, and you hemo clothes at night. One sip of this potent cocktail will hemo pressure (pronounced "presha") of a long, hard day's work.

$^1/_2$ **cup ice**

1 tablespoon frozen passion fruit juice concentrate

2 tablespoons canned unsweetened coconut milk

2 tablespoons coconut syrup, or 4 tablespoons Coco Lopez

1 tablespoon Malibu coconut-flavored rum

1 tablespoon Myers's dark rum

1 tablespoon 151 proof rum

1 maraschino cherry

1 mint sprig

1 pineapple wedge, for garnish

In a blender, combine the ice, passion fruit juice, coconut milk, coconut syrup, and rums and purée until smooth. Pour into a hurricane glass. Add the cherry and mint sprig. Garnish the glass with the pineapple wedge.

YIELD: I COCKTAIL

Basics

Basics

The recipes and techniques in this chapter form the foundation for many of the recipes in this book. Use them as building blocks for recipes from various cuisines and for your own creations as well.

Slivered Scallions

These very finely julienned scallions make an excellent, all-purpose garnish. They provide both color and a hint of Asian flavor. Since many of the recipes in this book call for the white parts of scallions, this makes an excellent and practical use for the green parts.

1 bunch scallions, green parts only

Using the back of a large, sharp knife, flatten the green parts of the scallions. Cut very finely on a diagonal so that the slivers are about 1 inch long.

YIELD: ABOUT $^1/_4$ CUP

Roasted Garlic

Roasting transforms the pungent flavor of garlic to give it a mellower, sweeter flavor.

1 head garlic
1 teaspoon olive oil
Salt to taste

Preheat the oven to 300°. Lightly rub the garlic with the olive oil. Season with salt. Place in a roasting pan. Roast for 1 hour. When cool enough to handle, halve the garlic crosswise and squeeze the soft garlic out of the cloves and into a bowl. Refrigerate in an airtight container for up to 1 week.

YIELD: ABOUT 3 TABLESPOONS

Chiles were introduced to Hawaii by Portuguese immigrants in the nineteenth century.

Chile Pepper Water

Instead of salt and pepper, you will find two bottled condiments on the tables at Alan Wong's: Chile Pepper Water and soy sauce. The same is true in many eateries in Hawaii—such are local tastes. We use this all-purpose condiment in a number of recipes for its subtle flavor and heat. It will keep for at least 1 month in the refrigerator.

$^1/_3$ cup plus 1$^1/_4$ cups cold water
$^1/_2$ clove garlic
2 red Hawaiian chiles or red serrano chiles, or 1 red jalapeño, halved and seeded
1 tablespoon white vinegar
2 teaspoons minced ginger
Pinch of salt

In a blender, combine the $^1/_3$ cup of water, garlic, chiles, vinegar, ginger, and salt and purée until smooth. In a saucepan, bring the 1$^1/_4$ cups of water to a boil. Add the puréed mixture and return to a boil. Remove from the heat. When cool, transfer to an airtight container. Keep refrigerated.

YIELD: 1$^1/_2$ CUPS

Five-Spice Broth

This broth is a key component of the Five-Spice Risotto (page 138) and the Chinatown Roasted Duck (page 111), and it makes a tasty soup all on its own. Add noodles and some vegetables, and you've got a great lunch.

8 cups Chicken Stock (page 177)
1 roast duck carcass, broken into pieces
$^1/_2$ cup chopped scallions, green and white parts
$^1/_2$ cup quartered shiitake mushrooms
1 (3-inch) piece of ginger, smashed
4 cloves garlic, halved
7 star anise
1 cinnamon stick
$^1/_2$ teaspoon fennel seeds
$^1/_2$ teaspoon coriander seeds
12 cloves
Salt and pepper to taste

In a stockpot over low heat, combine the stock, duck carcass, scallions, mushrooms, ginger, garlic, star anise, cinnamon, fennel, coriander, and cloves. Simmer for 2 hours. Remove from the heat and strain. Season with salt and pepper.

YIELD: ABOUT 6 CUPS

Tomato Water

I created this recipe because I did not want to waste the tomato ends and trimmings or prepared tomatoes that we often had on hand at the end of the day. Using a filter and letting the tomatoes drip, rather than just pressing or blending them, results in a clear colorless liquid. Its subtle acidity brings out other flavors, which is advantageous when combined with other ingredients.

5 tomatoes, coarsely chopped
1$^1/_2$ tablespoons salt

In a blender, combine the tomatoes and salt and blend until smooth. Pour into a strainer lined with a disposable coffee filter or cheesecloth placed over a bowl. Refrigerate to drain overnight; do not press.

Remove the filter paper and reserve the tomato pulp for another use. Keep the strained liquid refrigerated.

YIELD: 2$^1/_4$ CUPS

Infused Tomato Water

This flavored version of Tomato Water gives an aromatic quality and a subtle zing to many dishes.

Tomato Water (this page)
1 tablespoon Chile Pepper Water (page 175)
2 cloves garlic, thinly sliced
6 fresh basil leaves
4 or 5 thin slices fennel bulb
Salt and pepper to taste

To the strained tomato liquid, add the Chile Pepper Water, garlic, basil, and fennel. Season with salt and pepper. Refrigerate for at least 1 hour to allow the flavors to develop. Transfer to an airtight container. Keep refrigerated.

YIELD: 2$^1/_2$ CUPS

Lobster Stock

This delicately flavored stock uses lobster heads, which are usually discarded when preparing lobster dishes. Make this stock whenever you have the heads available and freeze it until needed. Alternatively, ask your fishmonger to save lobster heads for you.

3 lobster heads
3 tablespoons vegetable oil
1/4 cup brandy
1/4 cup sliced celery
2 tablespoons sliced carrot
1/2 cup chopped onion
1 small head garlic, halved crosswise
1 1/2 cups tomato paste
1 pinch saffron
1/2 tablespoon black peppercorns
2 sprigs thyme
2 bay leaves
4 quarts Chicken Stock (this page)

Halve the lobster heads lengthwise and remove the stomach. In a sauté pan over high heat, heat 2 tablespoons of the oil unitl hot. Sear the heads for 2 minutes, turning often. Transfer the heads to a stockpot. Add the brandy to the sauté pan, taking care as the alcohol will ignite. When the flames expire and the alcohol has burned off, deglaze the pan and add the pan drippings to the stockpot.

Reduce the heat under the pan to medium-high. Add the remaining 1 tablespoon of oil. When hot, add the celery, carrot, and onion. Sauté until browned. Add to the stockpot.

Add the garlic, tomato paste, saffron, peppercorns, thyme, bay leaves, and stock and bring to a boil. Reduce the heat to low and simmer for about 2 hours, occasionally skimming any impurities that rise to the surface. Transfer in batches to a blender or food processor and blend again. Strain. Refrigerate for up to 5 days, or freeze for up to 3 months.

YIELD: ABOUT 2 1/2 QUARTS, OR 10 CUPS

Chicken Stock

Never underestimate the importance of a good stock or your ability to make great stocks. If you master the art of stock making, you have what it takes to prepare great soups and spectacular sauces. Remember that the stock pot is neither a rubbish can nor a catchall. If you treat it with respect and use quality ingredients, the results will speak for themselves.

2 1/2 pounds chicken bones, rinsed
5 quarts water
1 small onion, chopped
1 stalk celery, sliced
1 small leek, sliced
1 small head garlic, halved crosswise
1/4 cup mushroom stems
1 sprig thyme
2 bay leaves
1/2 teaspoon black peppercorns

In a stockpot over medium heat, combine the bones, water, onion, celery, leek, garlic, mushrooms, thyme, bay leaves, and peppercorns and bring to a boil. Reduce the heat to low and simmer for 2 hours, occasionally skimming any impurities that rise to the surface. Remove from the heat and strain. Refrigerate for up to 5 days, or freeze for up to 3 months.

YIELD: ABOUT 4 QUARTS, OR 16 CUPS

Fish Stock

For best results, use scraps and bones of non-oily, white-fleshed fish such as moi, flounder, sole, or halibut.

2 1/2 pounds fish scraps and meaty bones
1 cup white wine
3/4 cup sliced celery
3/4 cup sliced leeks
1 1/2 cups chopped onions
1/2 cup mushroom stems and pieces
1/2 cup tomato scraps or diced tomato
1 small head garlic, halved crosswise
3 sprigs thyme
2 bay leaves
1/2 tablespoon black peppercorns
2 sprigs flat-leaf parsley
3 quarts water

In a stockpot over low heat, combine the fish and wine. Simmer gently for 10 minutes. Increase the heat to medium-high. Add the celery, leeks, onions, mushrooms, tomato, garlic, thyme, bay leaves, peppercorns, parsley, and water. Reduce the heat to low and simmer for 45 minutes, occasionally skimming any impurities that rise to the surface. Remove from the heat and strain. Refrigerate for up to 5 days, or freeze for up to 3 months.

YIELD: ABOUT 2 QUARTS, OR 8 CUPS

Lamb Stock

See the notes for the Veal Stock (page 179), which apply equally to this flavorful stock.

3 pounds lamb bones
1 1/2 cups coarsely chopped onions
3/4 cup coarsely chopped celery
3/4 cup coarsely chopped carrots
3/4 cup mushroom stems and pieces (optional)
1 bulb garlic, halved crosswise
1 tomato, coarsely chopped
5 tablespoons tomato paste
1/4 cup coarsely chopped fresh flat-leaf parsley
5 sprigs thyme
2 bay leaves
1/2 tablespoon black peppercorns
1/2 cup red wine
5 quarts water

Preheat the oven to 500°. Place the bones in a large roasting pan and roast for 30 to 40 minutes, or until browned. Place the onions, celery, and carrots in a separate roasting pan and roast for 20 to 25 minutes, or until well caramelized. In a stockpot over low heat, combine the bones, caramelized vegetables, mushrooms, garlic, tomato, tomato paste, parsley, thyme, bay leaves, and peppercorns. Add the wine to the roasting pan, deglaze the pan, and add the pan drippings to the stockpot. Add the water and simmer for 6 to 8 hours. Remove from the heat and strain. Refrigerate for up to 5 days, or freeze for up to 3 months.

YIELD: ABOUT 2 3/4 QUARTS, OR 11 CUPS

Lamb Jus

You will need to make the Lamb Stock before making this jus.

3 cups Lamb Stock (this page)
2 teaspoons butter
2 teaspoons flour

In a saucepan, bring the stock to a boil. Reduce the heat to medium. Cook until the stock is reduced to 2 cups. In a separate saucepan over medium heat, melt the butter and whisk in the flour. Keep whisking for 2 to 3 minutes, or until thoroughly combined and pastelike. Gradually whisk in the hot stock and continue whisking until well incorporated and slightly thickened.

YIELD: ABOUT 2 CUPS

Veal Stock

You can use fewer veal bones for the stock recipe, but its flavor will be less intense. Add more water as necessary to keep the bones covered in the stockpot. Reduce the strained stock for a more concentrated flavor.

2^1/$_2$ **pounds veal bones**

1^1/$_2$ **cups coarsely chopped onions**

^{3}/$_4$ **cup coarsely chopped celery**

^{3}/$_4$ **cup coarsely chopped carrots**

^{3}/$_4$ **cup coarsely chopped mushroom stems and pieces**

1 **small bulb garlic, halved crosswise**

6 **tablespoons tomato paste**

^{1}/$_3$ **cup coarsely chopped fresh flat-leaf parsley**

2 **sprigs thyme**

1 **bay leaf**

^{1}/$_2$ **tablespoon black peppercorns**

6 **tablespoons red wine**

3 **quarts water**

Preheat the oven to 500°. Place the bones in a large roasting pan and roast for 30 to 40 minutes, or until browned. Place the onions, celery, and carrots in a separate roasting pan and roast for 20 to 25 minutes, or until well caramelized. In a stockpot over low heat, combine the bones, caramelized vegetables, mushrooms, garlic, tomato paste, parsley, thyme, bay leaf, and peppercorns. Add the wine to the roasting pan, deglaze the pan, and add the pan drippings to the stockpot. Add the water and simmer for 6 to 8 hours. Remove from the heat and strain. Refrigerate for up to 5 days, or freeze for up to 3 months.

YIELD: ABOUT 2^1/$_2$ QUARTS, OR 10 CUPS

Veal Jus

You will need to make the stock before making the jus.

3 **cups Veal Stock (this page)**

2 **teaspoons butter**

2 **teaspoons flour**

In a saucepan, bring the stock to a boil. Reduce the heat to medium. Cook until the stock is reduced to 2 cups. In a separate saucepan over medium heat, melt the butter and whisk in the flour. Keep whisking for 2 to 3 minutes, or until thoroughly combined and pastelike. Gradually whisk in the hot stock and continue whisking until well incorporated and slightly thickened.

YIELD: ABOUT 2 CUPS

Ginger-Scallion Oil

Childhood memories of cold Chinese ginger chicken inspired this recipe. It is another versatile oil that can be drizzled over grilled foods as a condiment, strained and used as a vinaigrette, or mixed with Aioli (page 182) to make a great bread spread. We also use it as a component in several recipes.

1/4 cup finely minced ginger
1/4 cup minced scallions, green parts only
1/4 cup peanut oil
1/4 teaspoon dark sesame oil
Pinch of salt

Place the ginger and scallions in a deep mixing bowl. In a small saucepan, heat the peanut oil until just smoking. Slowly pour the hot oil over the ginger and scallion, being very careful as the oil will rise up the sides of the bowl. Add the sesame oil. Season with salt. Keep refrigerated.

YIELD: 3/4 CUP

Chile Oil

Like the other oils in this chapter, this flavorful piquant oil makes a great gift, especially if you use an attractive glass bottle.

1/2 cup chile paste with garlic (preferably Sambal Oelek)
1/2 cup olive oil
1/3 cup macadamia nut oil
8 dried Hawaiian red chiles or dried tepin or pequin chiles

In a blender, combine the chile paste and olive oil and blend for 2 minutes. Place a coffee filter in a fine mesh strainer and, in the refrigerator, strain the oil blend into a mixing bowl. Let sit for at least 1 hour. Remove the strainer and discard the filter. Add the macadamia nut oil to the bowl and mix well. Pour into a glass bottle with a cork or cap and add the dried chiles. Seal and keep refrigerated.

YIELD: ABOUT 1 1/3 CUPS

Asian Oil

This clear, bright green oil is the perfect pantry item to have on hand when you need to accent salads or other foods with distinctively Asian flavors.

1 cup firmly packed spinach
1/2 cup firmly packed fresh basil
1/4 cup firmly packed cilantro
1 1/2 cups olive oil
2 tablespoons Chile Pepper Water (page 175)
1 tablespoon Thai fish sauce
1 tablespoon freshly squeezed lime juice
12 kaffir lime leaves
2 tablespoons minced lemongrass
1 tablespoon minced ginger
1 tablespoon minced garlic
1 red serrano chile, chopped (optional)
Salt and pepper to taste

In a saucepan of boiling salted water, blanch the spinach, basil, and cilantro for 5 seconds. Drain and transfer to an ice bath to cool. Drain again and transfer to a blender. Add the oil, Chile Pepper Water, fish sauce, lime juice, lime leaves, lemongrass, ginger, garlic, and chile. Season with salt and pepper and purée; do not overblend as the oil will lose its color. Strain through a very fine sieve or strainer so that the oil is clear and bright green. Store in a glass container in a cool, dark place for up to 3 months.

YIELD: 1 3/4 CUPS

Basil Oil

This intensely aromatic and flavorful all-purpose oil brings the essence of summer to the plate. Its attractive green tint also makes it quite decorative.

$^1/_4$ **cup firmly packed spinach leaves**
$^1/_2$ **cup firmly packed fresh basil leaves**
1 tablespoon freshly squeezed lemon juice
$^1/_2$ **tablespoon Chile Pepper Water (page 175)**
$^1/_2$ **tablespoon minced garlic**
$^3/_4$ **cup olive oil**
Salt to taste

In a saucepan of boiling salted water, blanch the spinach for 5 seconds. Drain and transfer to an ice bath to cool. Drain again and transfer to a blender. Add the basil, lemon juice, Chile Pepper Water, garlic, and oil. Season with salt, place in a blender, and purée; do not overblend as the oil will lose its color. Strain through a very fine sieve or strainer so that the oil is clear and bright green. Store in a glass container in a cool, dark place for up to 3 months.

YIELD: I CUP

Garlic Butter

If you like garlic, then you'll want to keep this all-purpose butter on hand at all times. Use it to top anything straight off the grill and, of course, as a delicious spread for crusty bread.

$^3/_4$ **cup butter, at room temperature**
2 tablespoons freshly squeezed lemon juice
$^1/_4$ **cup white wine**
$^1/_4$ **cup minced garlic**
Salt to taste

In a bowl, thoroughly combine the butter, lemon juice, wine, and garlic. Season with salt. Refrigerate, wrapped in waxed paper, for up to 1 month, or freeze.

YIELD: I$^1/_4$ CUPS

Green Butter

This is another flavored savory butter that you will want to keep in the refrigerator or freezer to perk up any cooked fish or shellfish. I use it for the corn side dish that accompanies the braised veal (page 116), and it's a must with escargots.

$^1/_2$ **cup butter, at room temperature**
1 teaspoon minced garlic
2 tablespoons minced fresh flat-leaf parsley
1$^1/_2$ tablespoons minced shallots
$^1/_3$ **teaspoon salt**
$^1/_8$ **teaspoon pepper**

In a bowl, thoroughly combine the butter, garlic, parsley, shallots, salt, and pepper. Refrigerate, wrapped in waxed paper, for up to 1 month, or freeze.

YIELD: $^3/_4$ CUP

Thyme and Red Bell Pepper Butter

This recipe, which I use for the Mushroom-Stuffed Lobster (page 62), is inspired by Christian Bertrand, the chef de cuisine at Lutèce in New York. When we began working together, I quickly developed a great admiration for Christian's cooking. One day he made this butter for a dish that featured—ironically—Hawaiian prawns.

1 cup butter, at room temperature
2 tablespoons freshly squeezed lemon juice
1/4 cup minced fresh thyme
2 tablespoons chopped fresh flat-leaf parsley
1/2 cup roasted, peeled, and minced red bell pepper
1/4 cup minced garlic
Salt to taste

In a bowl, combine thoroughly the butter, lemon juice, thyme, parsley, bell pepper, and garlic. Season with salt. Refrigerate, wrapped in waxed paper, for up to 1 month, or freeze.

YIELD: 2 CUPS

Beurre Blanc

This classic French butter sauce provides a pleasing contrast to the Asian flavors found in many of our dishes.

1 cup white wine
1/4 cup white wine vinegar
3 tablespoons minced shallots
3 white peppercorns, crushed
1/2 cup heavy cream
1/2 pound cold butter, cut into 8 pieces
Salt and white pepper to taste

In a saucepan over medium-high heat, bring the wine, vinegar, shallots, and peppercorns to a boil. Cook until the liquid is reduced to about 1/4 cup. Add the cream, return to a boil, and cook until again reduced to 1/4 cup (the mixture will be thick enough to coat the back of a spoon). Remove from the heat and whisk in the butter, allowing each piece of butter to melt before adding more, until it is all incorporated. Season with salt and pepper and strain into a clean saucepan.

YIELD: I CUP

Aioli

The classic Provençale aioli is a garlic-flavored mayonnaise. This version gets a little boost with the addition of Dijon mustard. This and the other aiolis in this chapter will keep in the refrigerator for up to 1 week. *Recipes containing uncooked eggs are not recommended for immuno-compromised individuals or small children.*

1 teaspoon Dijon mustard
1 teaspoon minced garlic
1 egg plus 1 yolk
1 tablespoon freshly squeezed lemon juice
1 cup olive oil
Salt and pepper to taste

In a blender, combine the mustard, garlic, egg, egg yolk, and lemon juice and purée. With the machine running, slowly add the olive oil until incorporated. If the mixture becomes too thick, thin with a little water. Season with salt and pepper. Keep refrigerated.

YIELD: I 1/2 CUPS

Chile Pepper Aioli

At Alan Wong's, we offer this condiment in a little ramekin to accompany our crusty dinner rolls. It makes a nice change from the usual butter, and it's ideal for the home table, too.

¹/₄ cup Aioli (page 182)
¹/₈ teaspoon cayenne, or to taste

In a bowl, thoroughly combine the Aioli and cayenne. Keep refrigerated.

YIELD: ¹/₄ CUP

Sambal Aioli

Here is another take on the spicy aioli theme, proving that aioli makes a great medium for other flavors, including those from Asia.

1 cup Aioli (page 182)
1 teaspoon chile paste with garlic (preferably Sambal Oelek)

In a blender, thoroughly combine the Aioli and chile paste. Keep refrigerated.

YIELD: I CUP

Soy-Mustard Aioli

Unusual as it sounds, soy sauce and mustard are wonderfully complementary partners. I use them together in sauces and as a drizzle. This aioli is particularly well-suited to dishes with Asian ingredients.

2 tablespoons mustard powder
2 tablespoons warm water
4 teaspoons Yamasa soy sauce or other brand
1 cup Aioli (page 182)

In a small stainless steel bowl, mix the mustard powder and water to form a smooth paste. Stir in the soy sauce. Add the Aioli and mix thoroughly. Keep refrigerated.

YIELD: I ¹/₃ CUPS

Hawaiian Chile Pepper Sour Cream

Cool sour cream and hot chile, combined here in well-balanced proportions of fats and acid, make lively flavor contrasts that satisfy the palate.

1 cup sour cream
1 red Hawaiian chile or red serrano chile, minced
1 tablespoon Chile Pepper Water (page 175)
1 tablespoon freshly squeezed lime juice
Salt to taste

In a blender, combine half of the sour cream, the chile, Chile Pepper Water, and lime juice. Blend together and transfer to a bowl. Fold in the remaining sour cream. Season with salt. Keep refrigerated for up to 1 week.

YIELD: I CUP

Simple Syrup

1¹/₃ cups water
¹/₂ cup corn syrup
2¹/₄ cups sugar

In a saucepan, bring the water, corn syrup, and sugar to a boil. Boil for 5 minutes, strain, and cool.

YIELD: 4 CUPS

GLOSSARY

Amaranth Leaves: The decorative edible leaves of the amaranth plant, originally native to Central America, are used as garnish and as salad greens.

Arborio Rice: Italian rice with high starch content is ideal for creamy risottos.

Banana Leaves: Particularly popular in the Philippines for wrapping a variety of foods and in Southwestern and Mexican cooking for wrapping tamales. Traditionally, banana leaves are used in Hawaiian cooking for wrapping and for covering the pig in the imu (see page 5). Available in squares in the freezer section of Latin and Asian markets.

Bok Choy: Also known as *pak choy* and Chinese white cabbage. This cruciferous vegetable has dark green leaves with a white stem.

Celeriac: Also known as celery root. This particular type of celery is grown specifically for the brown-skinned, roundish root. It has crunchy white flesh and flavor similar to celery.

Chile, Red Hawaiian: Small fresh red chiles with strong heat. Substitute red serrano chiles or red jalapeños.

Chinese Five-Spice Powder: A blend in equal parts of ground clove, cinnamon, star anise, fennel, and Szechuan peppercorns.

Chipotle Chile: Dried, smoked jalapeño chile. Available in dried form or canned in a spicy sauce from Latin markets.

Chiso: A Japanese herb also called perilla or beefsteak mint. Chiso, sometimes spelled "shiso," is the ultimate palate cleanser and particularly good with fish. Grow in a window-box or herb garden for a reliable source. Available in Asian markets, or ask your local Japanese sushi bar or restaurant for chiso leaves.

Choy Sum: Also known as yo choy and similar to gai lan (Chinese broccoli). Substitute spinach or mustard greens.

Daikon: Long white Japanese radish with crisp juicy flesh and a mild flavor.

Enoki Mushrooms: Also known as enokitake. Tiny white mushrooms sold in clumps. Trim the roots before use.

Furikake: Japanese seasoning mix usually consisting of dried bonito (tuna) flakes, dried seaweed, ground sesame seeds, and salt.

Haricots Verts: Also known as French beans. An exceptionally thin, stringless green bean.

Haupia: Traditional Hawaiian dessert made with coconut milk and arrowroot or cornstarch (see page 155).

Hearts of Palm: Tender center of peach palm stems. Increasingly available in the preferable fresh form. Substitute canned hearts of palm, but the flavor is quite different (see page 80).

Hoisin Sauce: Rich, thick, and spicy-sweet sauce made from fermented soybean paste, garlic, vinegar, sugar, and seasonings. Refrigerate after opening.

Inamona: Traditional Hawaiian seasoning made with toasted ground kukui nuts (see page 55).

Ja-Chai: Chinese pickled cabbage, available at Asian markets. Use as a condiment with rice, like the Korean kim chee, and in stir-fries and soups. It tastes salty and slightly spicy with a crunchy texture. Substitute fresh Chinese mustard cabbage (kai choy).

Kaffir Lime Leaves: Fresh or dried leaves of a Thai citrus (also grown in Hawaii) used for flavoring. Rehydrate dry leaves. Like bay leaves, remove the leaves before serving.

Kiaware Sprouts: Daikon radish sprouts with a pungently spicy flavor.

Lemongrass: A tall, fibrous grass resembling a scallion but with tougher skin. Aromatic lemony flavor. Trim the stalk and roots and use only the bottom half.

Limu: Type of edible seaweed, traditionally used as a seasoning in Hawaii.

Lumpia Wrappers: Large (8-inch square) thin wrappers made with flour or cornstarch, traditionally used for Filipino filled and deep-fried spring rolls.

Maui Onion: Sweet, mild, and delicious type of sweet onion grown in up-country Maui. Substitute other types of sweet onions.

Mirin: Also known as rice wine. Sweet sake with a syrupy texture used for cooking, especially sauces. Substitute sweet sherry, although the flavor is different.

Miso (white): Also known as shiro miso. Sweet, thick, and mild-flavored paste made from soybeans, often used in soups, sauces, and dressings.

Mizuna Lettuce: Delicate Japanese salad green with a slightly peppery taste, now grown in many parts of the United States. Used for Japanese New Year celebration.

Nori: Black, purple, or dark green paper-thin sheets of dried seaweed used to wrap sushi or musubi. Should be lightly toasted before use unless labeled *yakinori* (toasted nori). Also crumbled and used as garnish.

Ogo: Japanese word for a type of edible seaweed (see Limu).

Opihi: Small Hawaiian limpets (see page 51).

Oyster Sauce: Chinese concentrated brown sauce made with fermented oysters, water, and salt. Richly flavored. Refrigerate after opening.

Panko: Japanese-style coarse bread crumbs that give a crunchy texture to coated fried foods. Substitute regular unseasoned bread crumbs.

Pipikaula: Cured dried beef. The Hawaiian equivalent of beef jerky (see page 16).

Poi: Traditional Hawaiian staple made from pounded, steamed, or boiled taro (see pages 10 and 116).

Rice Wine Vinegar: Also known as rice vinegar. Light vinegar made with fermented rice wine. Available unseasoned, or seasoned with salt and other ingredients.

Saimin Noodles: Hawaiian-style noodle dish usually consisting of a broth with meat and vegetables.

Sake: Japanese fermented rice wine, clear in color, usually served warm. Also used extensively in Japanese cooking.

Salt: We prefer kosher salt, which has no additives, or Hawaiian rock salt. All measurement amounts for salt in this book are given for kosher salt. Otherwise, use less table salt to taste.

Sambal Oelek: A brand of chile paste with garlic and brown sugar, from Indonesia. Substitute similar sauces from another Asian country, such as Lan Chi. Refrigerate after opening.

Sesame Oil (Dark): Intensely flavored oil pressed from toasted sesame seeds. Not to be confused with the more neutral, light-colored sesame oil, made from untoasted seeds.

Shichimi Togarashi: Also known as hichimi. Dark red Japanese seasoning made with seven spices, including chile, sesame, nori, and tangerine peel. Available in mild, medium, and hot strengths.

Shiitake Mushrooms: Also known as golden oak mushrooms. Dense Japanese mushrooms with brown caps cultivated widely in the United States and available in both fresh and dried forms.

Soy Sauce: In Hawaii, soy sauce is usually called by its Japanese name, *shoyu*. Yamasa is my preferred brand because it is neither overpowering in flavor, oversalty, nor oversweet, unlike many other types. Yamasa brand is particularly well-suited to sushi.

Tamarind Paste: Made from the pods of the tamarind tree, this fruity-sour sticky paste is used for flavoring and seasoning.

Taro: A nutritious tuber and a staple food in ancient Hawaii, also used to make poi. The leaves are cooked as a vegetable green and used to wrap foods for steaming (see pages 10 and 135). Substitute yuca (cassava).

Tat Soi: Also known as flat cabbage. The shiny lollipop-shaped leaves are often included in mesclun mixes for their crisp, juicy texture. Makes a striking garnish.

Thai Basil: Southeast Asian basil with maroon-green leaves and a slightly spicy flavor. Substitute green or opal basil.

Thai Chile Sauce: Condiment made with chiles, salt, sugar, and vinegar. Sriracha is the most common brand, named after the village in Thailand where it is made.

Thai Fish Sauce: Also known as Nam Pla. Pungent, flavorful ingredient made from fermented anchovies. Fish sauce is also made in other Southeast Asian countries, but the Thai version is preferred.

Thai Red Curry Paste: Fiery bottled paste typically made with dried and fresh red chiles, cumin, coriander, ginger, garlic, cilantro, lemongrass, shrimp paste, and peanut oil.

Ti Leaves: Available at florists or in packages at Filipino and other Asian markets (see page 5).

Tobiko: Also known as flying fish caviar. Orange in color and mild in flavor. Available at Japanese markets, sushi bars, or specialty fish stores.

Tomatillos: Bright green, tartly flavored, plum-sized fruit that resemble small green tomatoes. Cultivated by the Aztecs and widely used in Mexican cooking.

Truffle Butter: Purchase truffle-flavored butter at specialty or gourmet food stores.

Ume Plums: Also known as ume-boshi. Salty, tart-flavored pickled Japanese plums. Also available in paste form and used as a seasoning.

Wasabi: Also known as Japanese horseradish. This green spicy condiment usually accompanies sushi and sashimi. If purchased in powdered form, mix with hot water for maximum pungency (see page 137). Also available in ready-made paste form. Peel and finely grate fresh wasabi root.

Wasabi Tobiko: Green tobiko seasoned with wasabi.

Water Chestnuts: Increasingly available fresh, which are preferable to canned (see page 131).

Won Bok: Also known as Chinese cabbage, napa cabbage, and celery cabbage. Crinkly pale green leaves and white stem with mild, juicy flavor. Use raw, blanched, or cooked.

Wonton Wrappers: Very thin square (or round) sheets made from a wheat flour and egg dough used to wrap foods such as dumplings, which are sometimes called "Asian ravioli." Cut the wrappers into thin strips and deep-fry for garnish.

Yuzu: Japanese lime juice. Yuzu is available bottled in Asian markets. If necessary, substitute fresh lime juice.

INDEX